All Rights Reserved. No part of this book may be reproduced in any form or by any electronic or mechanical means including information storage and retrieval systems without permission from its publisher, CFI Book Division.

Robert J. Wieland / Donald K. Short
Copyright CFI Book Division © 2025

Published by CFI Book Division
P.O. Box 159, Gordonsville, Tennessee 38563
ISBN: 979-8-9892954-1-8

"An Explicit Confession
 . . . Due the Church"

November 1972

Contents

"An Explicit Confession . . . Due The Church"	1
What Did The Authors Say In The Beginning?	4
The Call For A Confession	6
What Should Be Done?	7
What *Movement Of Destiny* Says	8
What Ellen G. White Says	9
Denominational Repentance?	14
Evidence Is Overwhelming ...	15
Does Ellen G. White Contradict Herself?	18
Is The Picture Balanced?	19
What Did The "Eyewitnesses" Really Say?	20
What About The "Confessions" Of Those Who Repented?	22
Can All Members Understand This Problem?	25
Did Re-organization Cancel Out Rejection?	25
What Attitude Did The Lord's Messenger Take?	30
The Honor And Vindication Of Christ Is Involved In This!	32
What Can We Say?	34
A Solution Must Be Found	36
Can Something Be Done?	38
Something Is Not Right!	38
Our "Confession"	41

Appendix A
    The New Testament Basis Of
            Corporate Guilt And Repentance 55

Appendix B
    "Fourteen-point Summation" Proving That
            The 'Jews' Accepted Christ as the Messiah 60

Appendix C
    Excerpts From *1888-Re-examined* 61

A Chronological Table Of Interest
    Leading To This "Confession" 64

About The Authors 70

Subject Index 72

Bibliography 74

Addendum 77

"AN EXPLICIT CONFESSION ... DUE THE CHURCH"

This public "confession" is made in response to a duty solemnly enjoined upon the authors of a private document. After twenty-two years of silence they are now required to speak publicly, though they would prefer to remain silent.

Their duty to "confess" is made clear by demands upon them published in *Movement of Destiny* and endorsed by the General Conference of Seventh-day Adventists.* It is a duty the authors dare not evade. The Church will expect a sincere response to such an authoritative public charge. Truth requires it.

Twenty-two years ago in the autumn of 1950 the authors prepared for the attention of the General Conference Committee a private manuscript entitled *1888 Re-examined*. Without the authors' consent or approval, this document with some 600 Ellen G. White exhibits was by others placed in the hands of an ever-widening circle of Seventh-day Adventist readers around the world. This is what has now been responsible for this public call to make "an explicit confession ... due the Church."

....

We said in 1950 that there is a neglected but essential preparation to make before the final outpouring of the Holy Spirit in the Latter Rain can possibly come to enable the Church to finish God's work on earth. That most necessary preparation is recognition of and repentance for the misunderstanding and rejecting the "beginning" of the Latter Rain and the Loud Cry. This "beginning," according to Ellen G. White, was a message brought by two young ministers to the 1888 General Conference Session. Nearly one hundred times in her writings she endorses this message and the messengers in language never used at any time about any other message or messengers.

For us now as a people to beg Heaven to give us the Latter Rain, without recognizing this obvious fact, is just as unreasonable as for the

---

* See *Movement of Destiny* (Washington, D.C.: Review and Herald Publishing Association 1971), pages 358, 364, 445, 451, 686, etc.

Jews to keep on begging the Lord to send them the Messiah without recognizing how He kept His promise and did send Him two thousand years ago.

Here are two examples of Ellen G. White's typical endorsement of the message:

> The, Lord in His great mercy sent a most precious message to His people through Elders Waggoner and Jones. This message was to bring more prominently before the world the uplifted Saviour, the sacrifice for the sins of the whole world. ... It is the third angel's message, which is to be proclaimed with a loud voice, and attended with the outpouring of His Spirit in a large measure.—TM 91, 92.

> The time of test is just upon us, for the loud cry of the third angel has already begun in the revelation of the righteousness of Christ, the sin-pardoning Redeemer. This is the beginning of the light of the angel whose glory shall fill the whole earth.—R&H, November 22, 1892.

Since the imperative demand was made in *Movement of Destiny* that we make a public "confession," we have spent much time in thought and prayer, considering what our response should be. We love the remnant church, we are a part of it, and our confidence in its ultimate triumph is strong. For the twenty-two years since we presented the original document to the General Conference Committee we have remained missionaries and ministers and have earnestly tried to carry out whatever assignments the church organization has given us, whether in Africa or in our homeland. We are grateful that the *Review and Herald* could say of us: "There has been no question on the part of the church leadership of the loyalty and sincerity of Elders Wieland and Short. ... They firmly support the organization and unity of the church."—R&H, May 8, 1969, pages 5, 6.

We have never supported or approved of any offshoot movement or disloyal element. It has been and is still our prayer that God's grace will sustain us in loyal service to Christ and His Church until He comes again.

There are many Seventh-day Adventists who have known little or nothing about that "beginning of the Latter Rain and Loud Cry" in 1888 or the real reason why the finishing of God's work has been delayed so many decades since. We are grateful that *Movement of Destiny* has told the church of the great importance of the 1888 Conference. We hope it enjoys wide readership. And we are especially glad that for the first time in history a major volume clearly confesses that the Lord gave through Elders Jones and Waggoner what was in reality "the beginning of the

Latter Rain" (see pages 262, 318, 321, 322, 325, 345, 570, 667, etc.). We see in this published call for us to make "an explicit confession" an indication of duty the Lord Himself has laid upon us. Through the years He has providentially placed in our hands a remarkable collection of unpublished Ellen G. White material that bears directly on the subject matter of this "confession." We believe that publication of this epochal volume by the Review and Herald Publishing Association will prove to be a major step toward bringing about those final events which will result in the finishing of God's work in this generation. We have waited many months beyond the publication of this book for the world field to have a chance to become acquainted with what it says. Now we must respond to its call.

What we said twenty-two years ago is brought into sharp focus and challenged by this book. As *Movement of Destiny* says the *1888 Re-examined* position is either "true, or not true." No compromise position is possible:

> If true, there should surely be some clear-cut *historical* evidence to definitely establish its validity. If it is true, there should be solid support for such a serious contention in the writings of the Spirit of Prophecy. But if it is merely personal opinion, or impression, or conjecture, it should be discounted and denied.—Page 358.

Surely this is a fair, right, and honorable approach to a serious problem. To this we agree. We also concur with the following:

> The facts are accessible. They are neither hidden nor ambiguous. The records of the time [1888 and since] are open and available. Our entire published literature is on record. ... And letters, diaries, and other communications have their bearing, together with decisive Spirit of Prophecy testimony. The latter constitute the determining factor.—*Idem*.

The authors certainly agree that "decisive Spirit of Prophecy testimony" must "constitute the determining factor." Though all men may speak otherwise, in the end the final judgment must be a "thus saith the Lord." And He "abhors indifference and disloyalty in a time of crisis in His work. The whole universe is watching with inexpressible interest the closing scenes of the great controversy between good and evil."

True Seventh-day Adventists have confidence in the writings of Ellen G. White. Therefore the inquiry must be put to them: Why has the finishing of God's work been so long delayed if the Latter Rain and the Loud Cry began in 1888? Did the Lord intend that world population should outgrow our witnessing efficiency? On January 9, 1893, the Lord's messenger said in very clear context that the work of God could have been finished *then* had the 1888 message been truly and heartily accepted:

> The Spirit of God has been present in power among His people, but it could not be bestowed upon them, because they did not open their hearts to receive it. ...
>
> The Lord designed that the messages of warning and instruction given through the Spirit to His people should go everywhere. But the influence that grew out of the resistance of light and truth at Minneapolis tended to make of no effect the light God had given to His people through the Testimonies. ...
>
> ... If every soldier of Christ had done his duty, if every watchman on the walls of Zion had given the trumpet a certain sound, the world might ere this have heard the message of warning. But the work is years behind. What account will be rendered to God for thus retarding the work? —*General Conference Bulletin*, 1893, page 419.

Let it be clearly understood that this statement is not quoted for the purpose of questioning the Lord's presence and blessing with His people for the past 80 years. He has been with them as truly as He was with Israel during their 40 years of wandering in the wilderness. The purpose of quoting this statement is to show that the *finishing* of God's work has been long delayed. And "we," not the Lord, are responsible!

We turn now to the subject matter of this "explicit confession" required from us.

WHAT DID THE AUTHORS SAY IN THE BEGINNING?

We stated our conviction in language none could misunderstand. Now after twenty-two years "clear-cut historical evidence" *must* "definitely establish its validity" *or* "it should be discounted and denied." The Lord's providence indicates that from now on the full facts must be open for the entire church to see. We summarize as follows what we said in 1950:

1. Between the 1860s and 1880s the Seventh-day Adventist Church was permeated by a legalistic, self-centered spirit that made the finishing of the gospel commission impossible in that generation. To correct the deficiency "the Lord in His great mercy sent a most precious message to His people" in the 1888 message of Christ's righteousness.

2. This message was far more than a mere re-emphasis of the historic Protestant 16th Century doctrine of "justification by faith" as taught by the Reformers. Our authoritative denominational histories up until 1950

had said that was all it was. The evidence is clear that the 1888 message was in reality the beginning of the Latter Rain and the Loud Cry. *We said so in 1950.*

3. Ellen G. White said over and over in words that to us proved that this 1888 message was misunderstood and rejected, not by the general laity but by the responsible leadership of the Church. This is why we as a people are still here with our task unfinished so many decades after the "beginning" of the final outpouring of the Holy Spirit, which was to have finished the gospel work *then* like fire goes in the stubble. Although "some" among the leadership accepted the 1888 message they are always said by Ellen G. White to be "few" while the rejectors are consistently said to be "many." And those "some" who accepted or wanted to accept were overborne by the impact of the determined opposition from men in responsible positions.

4. Further, we discovered abundant Spirit of Prophecy testimony declaring that the opposition to the 1888 message was enmity against Christ of the same nature as the enmity the Jews manifested against Him when they crucified Him. If ever a people on earth needed the "final atonement," we do. Thus "the cleansing of the sanctuary" can never be complete until the 1888 incident of our history is fully understood by the responsible leadership of the Church today and the tragic mistake rectified by this generation. This cleansing of the heavenly sanctuary requires a complementary and parallel work of cleansing the unconscious content of our heart and mind of those hidden, buried, "underground" roots of unbelief and enmity against God (and one another, too).

5. Our greatest need as a Church is spiritual, not numerical or financial. Even should we "baptize" millions more lukewarm, spiritually self-satisfied members, this is not *true* "progress." A contrite reconciliation with the Lord Jesus Christ is our need. Only then can true love permeate the Church.

6. The Lord has been with us truly in all our "wanderings" since 1888 just as He was with Israel during their wanderings in the wilderness long ago. The Church, enfeebled and defective as she is, is still the object of His supreme regard. We are not better than our "fathers." We cannot criticize a past generation for their refusal to accept the Latter Rain. But we can repent now as a generation and as a denomination, so that we shall not repeat their tragic mistake. "The long Detour of wandering which we brought upon ourselves must lead us in the fulness of the time to the Christ whom we spurned at Minneapolis. In self-abhorrence and

deep repentance, we shall find Him." This position requires absolute loyalty *both* to the Church and to Christ.

7. The self-centered motivation ("let's finish the work so we can all go home to glory") is not sufficient to arouse the Church to Christlike service. The real issue is the integrity and honor of God's throne. "He has staked that honor upon His confidence in the honesty of the Seventh-day Adventist conscience. In a sense, God Himself is now on trial in the course to be pursued by His people. ... If now [1950] is understood to be the time for the proclamation of the loud cry, it follows that *now* is the time for the making right of the [1888] wrong. The mistake of [1888] was the rejection of the very power which the church is now committed to a program of seeking for."

8. Therefore before the Lord can again pour out His Holy Spirit in full measure for finishing the gospel commission in all the world, the General Conference Committee must lead the Church in denominational repentance. Otherwise, there is grave danger in our determination to secure supernatural "power." In our false assumption that we truly accepted the 1888 message we have thought ourselves "rich and increased with goods, and in need of nothing" when we are really confused by Babylon's ideas of "righteousness by faith." These have largely taken the place of the truth the Lord sent us in 1888. Unless we accept our Lord's call to denominational repentance ("Be zealous therefore, and repent," Revelation 3:19), there is grave danger of our becoming infatuated with a false Christ and a false and counterfeit "holy spirit" which we can easily mistake for the true.

9. Such a situation is extremely serious. The first step in rectifying the prevailing confusion (1950) should be the publication of an anthology of the long out-of-print writings of the "messengers" whom the Lord sent in 1888.

So said the authors in 1950. A number of their original statements may be found in Appendix C.

THE CALL FOR A CONFESSION

The position we expressed so frankly in 1950 is what the authors are now urged to "confess," apologize for, and retract before the Church. *Movement of Destiny* requires from the authors this "confession" thus:

> ... Echoers still persist, maintaining that the leadership of the Movement, at that time, [1888] "rejected" the message of Righteousness by Faith, and thereby incurred the continuing disfavor of God.

And along with that assumption and assertion goes a contention that until and unless the *Movement as a whole today*—nearly eighty years later—repents as a body in sackcloth and ashes for the sins of the "some" who, back at that fateful time, did definitely reject the Minneapolis Message at and following 1888, the smile and benediction of God will never rest upon the Advent people and Movement, and its message will never be consummated under present conditions.

In other words, such maintain that the Loud Cry and Latter Rain will never be visited upon us until that retroactive penitence requirement is met through some official acknowledgement and action. ...

Such a contention is a grave charge for anyone to bandy about. ...

... If the charge be not true, an explicit confession is due the Church today by promulgators of a misleading charge, first of all against the names of the post-1888 leadership, now all sleeping. Moreover, it is likewise due those in the Church today who have been confused and misled by such an allegation. In the ultimate, then, it actually constitutes an impeachment of the dead. That is a gravely serious matter.—Pages 357, 358.

The entire issue is indeed "a gravely serious matter" and *one that needs to be settled* before the Church can come into the unity of the faith necessary for its final victory.

WHAT SHOULD BE DONE?

The two authors of *1888 Re-examined* and the author of *Movement of Destiny* agree that "decisive Spirit of Prophecy testimony ... constitutes the determining factor" in arriving at the truth of this matter as stated on page 358. Therefore what must be settled is the inclusion or exclusion of "decisive Spirit of Prophecy testimony" that is vital and relevant. By leaving out certain key testimony it becomes impossible to understand correctly the meaning of post-1888 Seventh-day Adventist history. By so doing, we are unprepared to face the critical and perilous future.

The Church will insist on seeing and must see that "decisive Spirit of Prophecy testimony." The call to denominational repentance stands or falls on whether or not "the leadership of the Seventh-day Adventist Church ... following the crisis of 1888" in heart truly accepted what Ellen G. White described as "the beginning of the Loud Cry." See *Movement of Destiny*, page 444. If they did truly accept it, then it becomes obvious that the Lord is responsible for the delay in finishing His work, and the present authors owe the Church an apology and retraction. If they did not truly accept it, then the Church is responsible for the delay in finishing the gospel commission, and we in this generation have something very definite to do to make matters right before we can seriously expect Heaven to pour out the Holy Spirit again.

WHAT *MOVEMENT OF DESTINY* SAYS

First consider the idea set forth in *Movement of Destiny* that the post-1888 leadership headed by President O. A. Olsen did truly accept the message. This point is vital because we are told that "we must ... look chiefly to him for determinative evidence" pages 358, 359. In other words, if the post-1888 General Conference President was clearly on the right side, it would be very likely that his administration was also on the right side. This is reasonable and fair. We agree that the General Conference President's record provides such "determinative evidence." Quoting in context as full and complete as possible, note what *Movement of Destiny* says:

> The nineties were marked by a succession of powerful revivals and helpful institutes—and confessions and a surrender to truth on the part of a growing majority of the Minneapolis disputants. ...
>
> ... These were tremendous gains.—Page 264.

The leading post-1888 mold on the Movement was, of course, largely given by the incoming General Conference president. We must consequently look chiefly to him for determinative evidence. Now, the record of Olsen's spiritual leadership is clear and loyal, and his definite support of, and undeviating leadership in, the broad field of Righteousness by Faith is openly before us.

> ... Olsen seemed to sense the spiritual bearings of the questions at issue, and gave quiet but effective leadership to their solution.
>
> ... Olsen's calm and kindly spirit helped to bind the Church together at this most difficult time, and to advance the Message of Minneapolis during those nine crucial years of his presidency following '88—that is, from 1888 to 1897. His was a healing, unifying, and helpful influence, following the tension of the stormy Session.
>
> ... The years of Olsen's administration saw a real revival and reformation ... Olsen's tenure of office was a time of awakening from Laodicean self-satisfaction and self-reliance, a renewal brought about

through the growing acceptance of the message of Righteousness by Faith. ...

So it cannot, with any show of right, be said that Olsen personally rejected or subdued the message of Righteousness by Faith, or led or aided or abetted in such a direction. Rather, those were the years of its steady early advance and spread. ...

Olsen diligently fostered various Ministerial Institutes in which Righteousness by Faith was stressed among our ministry. He fostered the study of the Spirit of Prophecy. ... That surely cannot be construed as rejection. Indeed, it was the precise opposite. ...

... Clearly, Olsen did *not* reject the message of Righteousness by Faith. ... Derogators of our *post*-1888 leadership have not, perhaps, thought this through.—Pages 358-364.

There are nearly fifty repetitions of these ideas in the book, some being the concurring opinions of other scholars and researchers cited. But the Church cannot help but discern that this vast and impressive repetition includes no vital Ellen G. White documentation.

WHAT ELLEN G. WHITE SAYS

Consider now the testimony of Ellen G. White. The extensive quotation in context is from a letter she wrote to Elder A. O. Tait dated August 27, 1896. This is eight years *after* Elder Olsen's administration began, giving plenty of time for adjustments and "confessions" to become effective (see *Movement of Destiny* pages 368-370). She describes in vivid language how the over-all leadership situation appeared to her:

Letter to Elder A. O. Tait, Battle Creek; "Sunnyside," Cooranbong, August 27, 1896.

Dear Brother: —

I have not written to you much because I knew that that which I should write you would only increase your burden and intensify the painful feelings you must have, while there is no hope that you can in any way relieve the situation.

I feel very sorry for Brother Olsen. I have written him much in regard to the situation. He has written back to me, thanking me for the timely letters, but he has not acted upon the light given. The case is a mysterious one. While traveling from place to place he has linked with him as companions men whose spirit and influence should not be sanctioned, and the people who repose confidence in them will be misled. But notwithstanding the light which has been placed before him for years in regard to this matter, he has ventured on, directly contrary to the light which the Lord has been giving him. All this confuses his spiritual discernment, and places him in a relation to the general interest, and wholesome, healthy advancement of the work, as an unfaithful watchman. He is pursuing a course which is detrimental to his spiritual discernment, and he is leading other minds to view matters in a perverted light. He has given unmistakable evidence that he does not regard the testimonies which the Lord has seen fit to give His people, as worthy of respect, or as of sufficient weight to influence his course of action.

I am distressed beyond any words my pen can trace. Unmistakably Elder Olsen has acted as did Aaron, in regard to these men who have been opposed to the work of God ever since the Minneapolis meeting. They have not repented of their course of action in resisting light and evidence. Long ago I wrote to A. R. Henry, but not a word of response has come from him to me. I have recently written to Harmon Lindsay and his wife, but I suppose he will not respect the matter sufficiently to reply.

From the light God has been pleased to give me, until the home field shows more healthful heart-beats, the fewer long journeys Elder Olsen shall make with his selected helpers, A. R. Henry and Harmon Lindsay, the better it will be for the cause of God. The far-away fields will be just as well off without these visits. The disease at the heart of the work poisons the blood, and thus the disease is communicated to the bodies they visit. Yet, notwithstanding the sickly, diseased state of things at home, some have felt a great burden to take the whole of believing bodies under their parental wings. ... It is not in the order of God that a few men shall manage the great interests throughout the field.

Many of the men who have acted as counselors in board and council meetings need to be weeded out. Other men should take their places; for their voice is not the voice of God. ... These men are no more called Israel, but supplanters. They have worked themselves so long, instead of being worked by the Holy Spirit, that they know not what spirit impels them to action.

The spiritual blindness which rests upon human minds seems to be deepening. ...

... It would have been much better to have changed the men on boards and committees than to have retained the very same men for years, until they supposed that their propositions were to be adopted without a question, and generally no voice has been lifted in an opposite direction. ...

      E.G. White

We heartily agree with the following from *Movement of Destiny*:

> Questions will be automatically answered as we painstakingly and open-mindedly survey the Ellen G. White witness. ...
>
> There is something here to anchor to—something dependable, authoritative, not marred by human misconceptions. We cannot safely go beyond Mrs. White in the revealed emphasis and positions set forth. Observance of this principle provides the safety and the certainty that we need today. And contrariwise, violation of this principle brings inevitable controversy, division, and variance.—Pages 445, 446.

Acceptance of this principle will indeed bring true and lasting unity. Nothing else will bring it. We would humbly emphasize that the only reason for any "variance" or "division" on this matter for many years has been that the dependable, authoritative revealed positions of Ellen G. White have not been open-mindedly surveyed, studied or accepted.

Do her *published* writings agree with this *un*published letter to Elder Tait? Does she contradict herself? We turn to a letter addressed to Elder O. A. Olsen dated May 1, 1895 as found in *Testimonies to Ministers*, pages 77-81. Twice in this letter those "some" who were resisting and "cultivating hatred" against the 1888 message are said as late as 1895 to be influential "men who are entrusted with weighty responsibilities" whose "satanic work" begun "at Minneapolis" is carried on by those who "have been holding positions of trust, and have been molding the work after their own similitude, as far as they possibly could." A year later she said:

> In Battle Creek you have evidence that men who have had the most to say are not walking with God. There is abundant activity, but not many are working in partnership with Christ; and those who walk and work apart from Him have been the most active in planning and inaugurating their methods.—TM 320, March 13, 1896.

Indeed, "some" were walking with the Lord truly. Were they "many" or "few"? What was the true relationship between those who believed the message and those who did not?

> I have tried to present the message to you as I have understood it, but how long will those at the head of the work keep themselves aloof from the message of God?—R&H, March 18, 1890.
>
> ... Just in proportion as men of influence close their own hearts and set up their own wills in opposition to what God has said, will they seek to take away the ray of light from those who have been longing and praying for light and for vivifying power. Christ has registered

all the hard, proud, sneering speeches spoken against His servants [Jones and Waggoner] as against Himself.—R&H, May 27, 1890.

In a letter to Elder Olsen dated June 4, 1896, Ellen G. White discloses that this same attitude was prevailing as late as then. She speaks 35 times of the reaction of "those in responsible positions" as still being resistance, rejection, despising, pouring contempt on, speaking against, unappreciating, refusing to accept, hating, not heeding, the "message," etc. etc.—TM 89-98. These are generic terms.

A third vital point of evidence is Ellen G. White's letter to Elder Olsen himself of May 31, 1896, which fully corroborates what she said to Elder Tait three months later. The context is unmistakable:

> I have communications which have been written for one and two years, but I have felt that for your sake they ought to be withheld until some one could stand by your side who could clearly distinguish Bible principles from principles of human manufacture, who, with sharp discernment could separate the strangely perverted, human imaginations, which have been working for years, from things of divine origin.
>
> I am sorry you have not regarded the warnings and instructions which have been given you, as of sufficient value to be heeded, but by disregarding them before men who care nought for them, have made them a common matter, not worthy to have weight in your practice. Your practice has been contrary to these warnings, and this has weakened them in the eyes of men who need correction, who in their life-practice have separated from God. ...
>
> Brother Olsen, you have lost much from your experience that should have been brought into your character building, by failing to stand firmly and faithfully for right, braving all consequences [the context of the letter is discussing the leadership resistance to the 1888 message]. Had you done this, you might have had a very different showing from what you now have. ...
>
> Scenes that were a shame to Christians, have been presented to me, as taking place in the council meetings held after the Minneapolis meeting. The loud voice of dispute, the hot spirit, the harsh words, resembled a political meeting more than a place where Christians were met for prayer and counsel. These meetings should have been dismissed as an insult to heaven. The Lord was not revered as an honored guest by those assembled in council, and how could they expect divine light to shine upon them; how could they feel that the presence of Jesus was molding and fashioning their plans? ...
>
> Brother Olsen, you speak of my return to America. For three years I stood in Battle Creek as a witness for the truth [1888-1891]. Those

who then refused to receive the testimony given me by God for them, and rejected the evidences attending these testimonies, would not be benefited should I return. ...

The Spirit of the Lord has outlined the condition of things at the Review and Herald offices. Speaking through Isaiah, God says, "I will not contend forever, neither will I be always wroth; for the spirit should fail before Me, and the souls which I have made. For the iniquity of his covetousness was I wroth, and smote him; I hid Me, and was wroth, and he went on frowardly in the way of his heart."

This is precisely what has been done in the offices of publication at Battle Creek.

Covetousness has been woven into nearly all the business transactions of the institution, and has been practised by individuals. This influence has spread like the leprosy, until it has tainted and corrupted the whole. ... The wrong principles remain unchanged. The same work that has been done in the past will be carried forward under the guise of the General Conference Association. The sacred character of the Association is fast disappearing. ...

To a large degree the General Conference Association has lost its sacred character, because some connected with it have not changed their sentiments in any particular since the Conference held at Minneapolis. Some in responsible positions go on "frowardly" in the way of their own hearts. Some who came from ... and from other places to receive an education which would qualify them for the work, have imbibed this spirit, carried it with them to their homes, and their work has not borne the right kind of fruit. The opinions of men, which were received by them still cleave to them like the leprosy; and it is a very solemn question whether the souls who become imbued with the spiritual leprosy of Battle Creek will ever be able to distinguish the principles of heaven from the methods and plans of men. The influences and impressions received in Battle Creek have done much to retard the work ...

... I have been shown that the people at large do not know that the heart of the work is being diseased and corrupted at Battle Creek.... I am called upon by the Spirit of God, to present these things before you, and they are correct to the life, according to the practice of the past few years. ...

God's work cannot be carried forward successfully by men, who, by their resistance to light, have placed themselves where nothing will influence them to repent or change their course of action."—Letter to O. A. Olsen, "Sunnyside," Cooranbong, N.S.W., May 31, 1896.

These are direct quotations from the Lord's inspired servant. They are dependable, authoritative, revealed positions of Ellen G. White and not private opinions injected to support an idea as to how the post-1888 denominational leadership reacted to the 1888 message.

A fourth statement of inspired evidence follows, indicating how the Lord's servant viewed the "real revival and reformation" and "advance [of] the Message of Minneapolis during those nine crucial years" (*Movement of Destiny*, pages 363, 362). She speaks in generic terms of "leaders" at "the heart of the work":

> Oh if I could have the joyful news that the will and minds of those in Battle Creek who have stood professedly as leaders, were emancipated from the teachings and slavery of Satan, whose captives they have been for so long, I would be willing to cross the broad Pacific to see your faces once more. But I am not anxious to see you with the enfeebled perceptions and clouded minds because you have chosen darkness rather than light. ...
>
> ... The heart of the work, the great center, has been enfeebled by the mismanagement of men who have not kept pace with their Leader. ... The whole body is sick because of mismanagement and miscalculation. The people to whom God has entrusted eternal interest, ... the keepers of light that is to illuminate the whole world, have lost their bearings.—Letter, February 6, 1896; *Special Testimonies for Ministers and Workers*, No. 10, pages 29, 30; TM 396, 397.

DENOMINATIONAL REPENTANCE?

Is it right that we as a people humble our hearts before the Lord? Does the watching universe see our present position in this light? Do they see our denominational history as a clear call to denominational repentance?

Movement of Destiny says emphatically, "No." It presents the post-1888 administration of O. A. Olsen as "chiefly" the "determinative evidence" supporting the "acceptance" and "revival/reformation" view. It also affirms it has the support of "some sixty of our ablest scholars," "experts," "key Bible teachers," "editors," and "veteran leaders." Could all these be mistaken in endorsing this popular view? Humanly speaking it would seem any volume with such "magnificent prepublication support" must be correct (see page 8). Yet we would earnestly ask, "What saith the Lord? What is the testimony of the Spirit of Prophecy?" Did the post-1888 denominational leadership truly accept that message which was said to be the "beginning" of the Latter Rain and the Loud Cry?

Through the last twenty-two years retired ministers and scholars, some of whom lived through this post-1888 era, have placed in our hands rare unpublished Ellen G. White material. Because we have known that it has not been policy to permit much of this highly pertinent material to be generally known, we have refrained from publishing it. But *Movement of Destiny* now says that "the facts are accessible. They are neither hidden nor ambiguous. The records of the time are open and available." Since this book now charges us with the duty of making "an explicit confession" publicly, the time has fully come to disclose what the Lord's servant said. Again we consult a private letter written near the close of Elder Olsen's nine-year term of office:

> I do not find rest in spirit. Scene after scene is presented in symbols before me, and I find no rest until I begin to write out the matter. I think we will institute, at least once each day, a season of prayer for the Lord to set things in order at the center of the work. Matters are being shaped so that every other institution is following the same course. The General Conference is itself becoming corrupted with wrong sentiments and principles. In the working up of plans, the same principles are manifest that have controlled Battle Creek for a long time. ... There will be no material change for the better until a decided movement is made to bring in a different state of things.—Letter, "Norfolk Villa," Prospect Street, Granville, N.S.W., Sept. 19, 1896.

EVIDENCE IS OVERWHELMING ...

"The Lord in His great mercy sent a most previous message to His people" in the 1888 message, a message that was intended to bring about the genuine revival and reformation of His people, and to swell into the "Loud Cry" (cf. TM 91). The people would have responded. There is no doubt about that. This is the true Church, and "Thy people shall be willing in the day of Thy power." What happened? We dare not theorize, or rationalize. In *1888 Re-examined* some 600 exhibits were used from the writings of Ellen G. White. Here is another one. This is also at present unpublished, and dated January 2, 1903, but it gives a direct answer, clear and unequivocal, as to what happened:

> For many years I have carried a heavy burden for our institutions. I have borne many messages from God. Yet I knew that those for whom these messages were intended were not heeding them. Sometimes I have thought I would attend no more large gatherings of our people, for my messages seem to leave little impression on the minds of our leading brethren after the meetings have closed, although I bear a

heavy burden, and go from the meeting pressed down as a cart beneath sheaves.

At this time when God's people should be bearing a plain, clear message, filled with earnestness and power, many who have been appointed to preach the truth are departing from the faith.— *Special Testimonies*, Series B. No. 6.

How could it be that the post-1888 leadership "diligently fostered various ministerial Institutes in which Righteousness by Faith was stressed [and] fostered the study of the Spirit of Prophecy" and yet in reality exerted an influence that "spread like the leprosy, until it has tainted and corrupted the whole"? (Compare *Movement of Destiny*, page 363 and Ellen G. White Letter, May 31, 1896.) The following letter to Elder O. A. Olsen, dated February 2, 1896, helps to answer this question:

> One night I was in Battle Creek [in vision of the night or dream], and was bearing a decided testimony to the church. I was invited to attend a committee meeting, but I said, "No, I cannot trust my message to your committees. Not all of those who compose your committees have a vital connection with God, and they will not comprehend the message that God has given me to bear. The church must hear my message, and I must speak in language that cannot be misinterpreted in the same way that messages have been misinterpreted again and again in Battle Creek, so that men have been led to turn from the counsel of God, and to follow their own ideas and imaginations. You have evaded the true meaning of the message."—"Norfolk Villa," Prospect Street, Granville, N.S.W., Feb. 2, 1896.

Consider now the very end of Elder Olsen's nine year administration. *Movement of Destiny* informs us that "*most of those who first took issue made confessions within the decade following 1888, and largely within the first five years, and thenceforth ceased their opposition. ... Only a small hard core of 'die-hards' continued to reject it. These left the faith.*" Pages 267, 268. But nearly a decade after 1888 Ellen G. White's view of the "revival and reformation" in Battle Creek is entirely different:

> To my brethren in Battle Creek:
>
> The work that will meet the mind of the Spirit of God has not yet begun in Battle Creek. When the work of seeking God with all the heart commences, there will be many confessions made that are now buried. I do not at present feel it my duty to confess for those who ought to make, not a general, but a plain, definite confession, and so cleanse the soul-temple. The evil is not with one man or two. It is the whole that needs the cleansing and setting in order.—Letter, "Sunnyside," July 27, 1897.

The General Conference Committee members themselves comprising the post-1888 leadership made the following confession on April 8, 1897:

> Several times of late the Lord has been obliged to state that His Testimonies have been really disregarded by those who thought they believed them. He says, "The reproofs and warnings from the Lord have been evaded, and interpreted and made void by the devices of men." One device to evade them, He says, was to "frame flimsy excuses." He says they were interpreted and made void, by men "putting their own construction upon them saying that they did not mean thus and so." He says—the Testimonies have been "argued away." He says, "They mean just as stated;" but that "those whom the Lord has warned, feel that the warning means something else; they explain it to signify the opposite of that which the Lord has said."—Statement of the General Conference Committee introducing *Special Testimonies for Ministers and Workers*, No. 9, April 9, 1897.

What were Sister White's true feelings about the spiritual history of the post-1888 leadership? We insist that *her* evaluation of the situation is far more accurate than anyone's opinions who did not have the gift of prophecy as she did. Bear in mind that the critical issue under discussion is the Lord's call to denominational repentance ("Be zealous therefore, and repent," Revelation 3:19). Is that call to repentance echoed in our 1888 history and does it vitally affect our preparation for the Latter Rain and Loud Cry? Another unpublished document that came into our possession years ago is the original unedited transcript of Ellen G. White's remarks made in the Battle Creek College Library on April 1, 1901, at 2:30 p.m. which presents clear-cut evidence:

> When we see that message after message that God has given, has been taken and accepted, but no change—just the same as it was before, then we know that there is new blood must be brought into the regular lines. ... Not that anyone means to be wrong, or to do wrong; but the principle is wrong, and the principles have become so mixed and so foreign from what God's principles are, and the message has been going constantly in regard to principles, sacred, holy, elevated, ennobling, in every institution, in the publishing house and in all the interest of the General Conference—everything that concerns the handling of the work, it requires minds that are worked by the Holy Spirit of God. ... There should be a renovation without any delay. ... This thing has been acted and reacted for the last fifteen years or more, and God calls for a change. ... Our standstill has got to come to an end; but yet every Conference, it is woven after the very same pattern. ... Enough has been said; enough has been said over

and over and over again, but it does not make any difference; they go right on just the same, professedly accepting it, but they do not make any change. Well, now, that is what burdens me; that is what burdens me. ... "You have lost your first love," you have lost it.

If we were asked, "Did the post-1888 leadership 'professedly accept' the 1888 message? " we would have to answer "yes." But "professedly accepting it" and "not making any change" will never finish God's work, even in a thousand years. It is this "professedly accepting it" which has confused certain sincere denominational historians into assuming that such lip service meant heart-acceptance. Isn't it time now to consider the truth?

DOES ELLEN G. WHITE CONTRADICT HERSELF?

The question may be asked: "These Ellen G. White statements do appear clear and convincing; but did she say other things that contradict these things? Are you withholding from the reader other Spirit of Prophecy material that says emphatically that the post-1888 leadership *did* truly accept the message which was to have been the beginning of the Latter Rain and the Loud Cry?" Ellen G. White was not given to contradicting herself. If there were such statements. *Movement of Destiny* would have published them. We have thus far in this "Confession" considered more relevant Ellen G. White material on this subject than is found in the entire 700 pages of *Movement of Destiny*. The context is given clearly in each instance. There is not the remotest possibility that the Lord's messenger contradicts the clear meaning that she herself presents in this abundant testimony.

The testimony is emphatic that those "some" who were on the Lord's side were "few." "Some" *did* accept and humbled their hearts in contrition and would have been ready to enter into the finishing of God's work in that generation; but they are always identified as "few" while the opposers among the leadership are as often identified as "many" or by the generic term "our brethren," or as "those in responsible positions in Battle Creek." In every instance where the word "many" refers to those who rejoiced in the 1888 message, the context indicates that they were lay members or younger ministers not in denominational leadership. Always in the full context are found expressions such as these:

> Our young men look to our older brethren, and as they see that they do not accept the message, but treat it as though it were of no consequence, it influences those who are ignorant of the Scriptures to reject the light. These men

who refuse to receive truth, interpose themselves between the people and the light.—R&H, March 18, 1890.

How long will those at the head of the work keep themselves aloof from the message of God? —*Idem*.

IS THE PICTURE BALANCED?

Another question may well be asked: "Are you authors giving us a balanced picture of this thing? Or are you painting too dark a picture of the real situation?"

We have seen that from 1888-1901 there was no true change in the spiritual attitude of the church leadership that made it possible for the Lord to renew His outpouring of the Latter Rain. The "testimony of Adventism's peerless witness," Ellen G. White, is so emphatic that there can be no question regarding its "balance." In fact, there is no "balance" between truth and error.

There never has been any question regarding the Lord's presence with His people during those dark years of wandering. In their original document of 1950 the authors emphasized their firm confidence in the Lord's presence with His people and His blessings on them from 1888 until now. They said:

> There are a few who wished to advance with Christ [in the post-1888 era] into the larger spiritual experiences of the finishing of the work, both in their own hearts and in the world. The general body (of leaders especially) were not ready. God had, therefore, to alter His purpose, and remain with His people. If they would not keep step with Him, He must at least keep step with them —*1888 Re-examined*, pages 124, 125, original document.

> The remnant church, enfeebled and defective as she is, is still the supreme object of His regard. The long Detour of wandering which we brought upon ourselves must lead us in the fulness of time to the Christ whom we spurned at Minneapolis. In self-abhorrence and deep repentance, we shall find Him.—*Ibid.*, p. 137.

In other words, our post-1888 era has been equivalent to Israel's forty years of wandering in the wilderness following their failure to enter the Promised Land at Kadesh-Barnea. All but two had to die in the wilderness, yet the pillar of cloud by day and pillar of fire by night failed not; God was with His people, but not in a program of conquering Canaan. In the same way the Lord has truly been with His people since 1888, but not in the outpouring of the Latter Rain and proclamation of the Loud Cry. Each generation has desperately tried to find evidence of the outpouring, but history has always pointed to the future.

WHAT DID THE "EYEWITNESSES" REALLY SAY?

The reader can see that Ellen G. White testimony is clear and consistent. But now a real problem arises. "Eyewitness and personal-participant attestations" referred to in *Movement of Destiny* appear on the surface to contradict her view (see pages 237-268). How could it be that these "twenty-six living participants at the 1888 Minneapolis Conference" in their "affidavits" give such a different picture?* For example, we are told, *"There was no denomination-wide, or leadership-wide rejection*, these witnesses insisted. The newly appointed leaders supported it. (C. McReynolds, Letter to L.E.F., April 25, 1930)."—*Movement of Destiny*, page 256, emphasis in original. This is indeed very perplexing! However, the reader is not permitted to see even one of these affidavits in context.** One has no way of knowing if all twenty-six contradicted Ellen G. White's view.

But the authors are certain that two of them did not, because copies of their eyewitness accounts came into their possession in 1949. Quoting directly:

> In 1888 I was sent as a delegate from the Kansas conference to the General Conference held that year in Minneapolis. ... I know that

---

* See *The Fascinating Story of Movement of Destiny*, Review and Herald Publishing Association, 1970, page 15.

** Neither is the reader permitted to see any significant previously unpublished Ellen G. White testimony in the entire 700 page volume. For example, when the "Testimony of Adventism's Peerless Witness," Ellen G. White, is at last brought to bear on this era, her actual "testimony" is almost completely omitted, though these two chapters occupy 21 pages. Indeed, about the only previously unpublished Ellen G. White material the reader is permitted to see is an excerpt from a letter to Mrs. Mary White on pages 673, 674. Dated November 4, 1888, the letter has no bearing on the outcome of the post-1888 leadership, the key issue. Astounding as it may seem, this one letter is virtually the only new contribution the reader receives from the Spirit of Prophecy. Nonetheless it is a significant letter. It does not support the position that "the rank and file of Seventh-day Adventist workers and laity accepted the presentations at Minneapolis and were blessed." It states: "My testimony ... has made the least impression upon many minds than at any period before in our history. ... I tremble to think what would have been in this meeting if we had not been here."

some of our dear brethren contend to this day that there was no confusion and really no debate. Well, I was there and was in the midst of it, both in the public meetings and in our private quarters [we were lodged in a large house with the delegation from Iowa], and I know the spirit of debate and controversy ran high and some very bitter feelings were developed, but the conference closed with a dark shadow over many minds. ...

I am sorry for anyone who was at the Conference in Minneapolis in 1888 who does not recognize that there was opposition and rejection of the message the Lord sent to His people at that time. It is not too late to repent and receive a great blessing.—C. McReynolds, *Experiences While at the General Conference in Minneapolis, Minn. in 1888.* White Estate D. File, 189.

Elder McReynolds went on to say that "most of the leading men who had refused the light at the Conference" came out "with clear confessions" "within two or three years." "Many, both ministers and people, were aroused and sought the Lord with sincerity of soul, and found light and peace." But did Elder McReynolds know of that steady stream of private correspondence from Australia that the reader of this "Confession" has now seen? Obviously not. Did he have prophetic insight to distinguish "professedly accepting it," to quote Ellen G. White's 1901 expression, from genuine heart-acceptance? Nowhere does Elder McReynolds suggest that the post-1888 leadership ever recovered the rejected "beginning" of the Latter Rain and the Loud Cry. Otherwise he could not have said in his day (1930), "It is not too late to repent and receive a great blessing."

The other eyewitness account that came into our possession is that of R. T. Nash (see *Movement of Destiny*, page 247). We will let him also speak for himself:

The writer remembers, and many who attended the meetings at that conference [1888] know of what took place at that conference meeting. When Christ was lifted up as the only hope of the church, and of all men, the speakers met *a united opposition from nearly all the senior ministers*. They tried to put a stop to this teaching of Elders Waggoner and Jones.—*An Eyewitness Report of the 1888 General Conference at Minneapolis*, Ellen G. White Publications Files, emphasis added.

This agrees fully with Ellen G. White's view of the matter. There remain twenty-four eyewitnesses yet to be heard from; but are we not conscience-bound to stand with the clear testimony of the one who was given the gift of prophecy?

WHAT ABOUT THE "CONFESSIONS" OF THOSE WHO REPENTED?

We are glad that for the first time in our denominational history *Movement of Destiny* boldly, officially, and clearly confesses that the 1888 message was the beginning of the Latter Rain and the Loud Cry. At last the Church can understand the problem of the long delay.

If those who rejected, or to use the milder but synonymous term "failed to accept," the beginning of the Latter Rain in 1888 later repented, why didn't the Loud Cry go forth with power during Elder Olsen's post-1888 administration? Why are we still here 80 years later? If his administration truly repented of rejecting the beginning of the Latter Rain, was the Lord implacable in withholding the full outpouring from the world? There can be no doubt about what really happened:

> ... Satan succeeded in shutting away from our people, in a great measure, the special power of the Holy Spirit that God longed to impart to them. The enemy prevented them from obtaining that efficiency which might have been theirs in carrying the truth to the world, as the apostles proclaimed it after the day of Pentecost. The light that is to lighten the whole earth with its glory was resisted, and by the action of our own brethren has been in a great degree kept away from the world.—Letter to Elder Uriah Smith, Letter 96, 1896, 1 SM 234, 235.

Notice the date: 1896—long after *all* the "confessions" had come in. Could Israel's experience at Kadesh-Barnea throw light on human nature to help us understand what happened? The Lord gave *them* the chance to conquer Canaan just as He gave *us* the opportunity to have part in the "Loud Cry" and see the work finished. Israel refused just as we refused. A long wandering began for them as it began for us in our history. Nevertheless, we read that the rejectors at Kadesh-Barnea confessed. Beautiful! Their confession was open and manly: "The people mourned greatly. And they rose up early in the morning, and gat them to the top of the mountain, saying, Lo, we be here, and will go up unto the place which the Lord hath promised: for we have sinned." Numbers 14:39, 40. "Now they seemed sincerely to repent of their sinful conduct." (PP 391.) But was it true and deep? We read further: "But they sorrowed because of the result of their evil course rather than from a sense of their ingratitude and disobedience. ... Their hearts were unchanged."

Now, we earnestly inquire: What does the Spirit of Prophecy say about the confessions of those who rejected the 1888 message? The lesson that emerges is so serious that it is time we learned it. The Lord offers a given generation of Church leadership *only one chance* to accept wholeheartedly the outpouring of the Latter Rain. By 1896 the brethren of that era had missed their glorious opportunity.

We turn again to consider the principles involved in the Kadesh-Barnea incident:

> The Lord still works in a similar manner to glorify His name by bringing men to acknowledge His justice. ... Confessions are made that vindicate the honor of God and justify His faithful reprovers, who have been opposed and misrepresented.—PP 393.

The "confessions" of the 1890s truly vindicate the 1888 message as being of God. Those who made them will, we hope, come up in the first resurrection. They died as honored workers. But *not one* had a part in giving the Loud Cry to the world; and *not one* was translated. And unless we learn our lesson in this generation, *we shall follow them to the grave.*

Ellen G. White rejoiced in their confessions. But let us see what she had to say about their spiritual discernment *after* they made them. Elder Smith confessed in early 1891; the following letter is dated two full years later. Mrs. White is speaking of him as the most prominent of the opposers, who exerted the strongest influence:

> The course pursued in this case [Elder Uriah Smith's recent renewed public opposition to Elder A.T. Jones) was the same as that taken at Minneapolis. Those who opposed Brethren Jones and Waggoner manifested no disposition to meet them like brethren, and with the Bible in hand consider prayerfully and in a Christlike spirit the points of difference. This is the only course that would meet the approval of God, and His rebuke was upon those who would not do this at Minneapolis. Yet this blind warfare is continued. ... It is an astonishment to the heavenly universe. ... Will my brethren tell me what spirit is moving them to action? ...
>
> The conference at Minneapolis was the golden opportunity for all present to humble the heart before God, and to welcome Jesus as the great Instructor; but the stand taken by some at that meeting proved their ruin. They have never seen clearly since, *and they never will;* for they persistently *cherish* the spirit that prevailed there, a wicked, criticizing, denunciatory spirit.
>
> ... Those who have been so stubborn and rebellious that they would not humble themselves to receive the light God sent in mercy to their souls, became so destitute of the Holy Spirit that the Lord could not use them. Unless they are converted, these men will never enter the

mansions of the blest.—Letter, George's Terrace, St. Kilda Road, Melbourne, January 9, 1893, emphasis added.

We sincerely hope that Elder Smith will enter "the mansions of the blest." But the point is not and never has been his individual and personal salvation after 1888. The point is: did he use his position to undo the influential damage he had done to the cause in rejecting the beginning of the Latter Rain? The above gives a true answer.

In an earlier letter to Elder Smith, Mrs. White was very frank. Speaking directly of the continuing opposition to the 1888 message, she said:

> God would have His people love one another and help one another, thus strengthening every good work. We should counsel with one another, the old experienced laborers with those whom God shall raise up to advance His work as we approach the great consummation [Jones and Waggoner as examples of the younger ones]. But if such men as Elder Smith, Elder Van Horn, and Elder Butler shall stand aloof, not blending with the elements God sees essential to carry forward the work in these perilous times, they will be left behind. ... The work will go forward; but these brethren, who have received the richest blessings, *will meet with eternal loss;* for though they should repent and be saved at last, *they can never regain that which they have lost* through their wrong course of action. They might have been God's instruments to carry the work forward with power; but their influence was exerted to counteract the Lord's message, to make the work appear questionable.—Letter, North Fitzroy, August 30, 1892, emphasis added.

Perhaps it will be appropriate to note in passing what the authors really did say 22 years ago about our brethren of a past generation:

> We may leave our dear brethren of a generation ago with their God. They sleep in the dust of the earth, and we trust they will awake in the first resurrection. There is no more need of their being lost, in the light of the findings of this chapter, than that the Israelites who died in the wilderness after being turned back from Kadesh-Barnea will not come forth in the first resurrection, their individual relationships to God determine that. But—Israel of that day could not enter alive into the Promised Land because of their unbelief. Neither could our brethren of a generation ago.
>
> Now we are on the stage. ... —*1888 Re-examined*, page 87, original document.

We are sure the Church cannot consider this an "impeachment of the dead."

CAN ALL MEMBERS UNDERSTAND THIS PROBLEM?

Some may wonder, "Can non-scholars sift this kind of evidence and arrive at the truth? Can laymen trust their judgment as they read the evidence? Isn't it 'a highly complex and confused problem' that must be left to 'experts'? "

The authors of this "Confession" believe that the familiar text applies in principle: "Write the vision and make it plain upon tables, that he may run that readeth it." Habakkuk 2:2. For many decades we have applied this to the ease with which the common man can understand the truth of the Sabbath, the prophecies, and other doctrine that make up Seventh-day Adventist teaching. We believe that Ellen G. White especially wrote in a lucid style that does not require "interpretation" and certainly not explaining away. Seventh-day Adventists are trained to evaluate evidence. Take the simple Sabbath truth, for example. There are some eight or ten New Testament texts that "scholars" superficially explain to support Sunday observance. Yet hundreds of thousands of Seventh-day Adventist layman have given up jobs in order to keep the seventh-day Sabbath, correctly evaluating the so-called "evidence." They have risked everything on their ability to understand a plain "Thus saith the Lord."

This matter is as simple and clear as the Sabbath truth. Brief excerpts out of context can be selected from Mrs. White's writings that may appear on the surface to support some particular viewpoint. But in the end the Seventh-day Adventist conscience will insist on seeing the full evidence, not someone's evaluation of what he judges it to be. The Church is capable of seeing and appreciating the truth. We agree with *Movement of Destiny* that the time has come when we must "weigh the evidence ... for the facts are accessible. They are neither hidden nor ambiguous" (page 358).

Our Lord's call to the Church and its leadership to "repent" is just as clear as any of our "doctrines" which have made us a people. It is not "new light" but is "old light" that has not been clearly perceived. The call is in Revelation 3, and has been there all along; and our denominational history affords an apt commentary to it.

DID RE-ORGANIZATION CANCEL OUT REJECTION?

Another question will occur to the thoughtful reader: "Granted that the post-1888 leadership never recovered what they lost by rejecting the beginning of the Latter Rain, and granted that they all had to go into their graves rather than enjoy the privilege of translation—did not the 1901

General Conference Re-organization cancel out the 1888 failure and undo the damage done in the previous thirteen years? Did not the 1901 Conference reverse the trend and bring in victory?" If the answer to this question is "yes," there is indeed no need for denominational repentance, and we owe the Church an apology as *Movement of Destiny* says.

The General Conference have recognized how important this question is. In 1966 the Review and Herald published a volume dedicated to the idea that the 1901 Conference did indeed reverse the trend and brought in "victory." The book was significantly titled, *Through Crisis to Victory 1888-1901*. The Foreword says:

> "The thirteen years between Minneapolis, 1888, and the General Conference session of 1901 were ... a period over which Providence could spell out the word *victory*."—Page 7.

The main purpose of writing the book was to counteract the influence which the circulation of *1888 Re-examined* had had throughout the world field. The author of *Through Crisis to Victory*,

> through interviews and correspondence, became acutely aware of the misleading conclusions that some Seventh-day Adventists had reached relative to the General Conference held in Minneapolis in the autumn of 1888, and the aftermath of that historic session. It was apparent that not a few had formed opinions based on fragmentary bits of information, and also that at times other major issues of the thirteen years following 1888 were mistakenly confused with the problems of that meeting.—Page 7.

It is abundantly clear that 1888 was the time of the "crisis" so far as *finishing the work of God in that generation* is concerned. That was the issue—receiving the Latter Rain and proclaiming the Loud Cry. To be perfectly honest, one must say that in that respect, 1888 was not only a "crisis," but defeat. We ask, as 1888 was in this respect "crisis," was 1901 really and truly "victory"?

Again we must turn to the actual testimony of the Spirit of Prophecy. A retired Conference president placed in our hands the following unpublished Ellen G. White correspondence which sets forth her retrospective views of the actual *results* of that 1901 Conference Session. What Ellen G. White says is distinctly different from the picture given in *Through Crisis to Victory*. She writes a year and a half later:

> Had thorough work been done during the last General Conference [1901] at Battle Creek; had there been as God designed there should be, a breaking up of the fallow ground of the heart, by the

men who had been bearing responsibilities; had they, in humility of soul, led out in the work of confession and consecration; had they given evidence that they received the counsels and warnings sent by the Lord to correct their mistakes, there would have been one of the greatest revivals that there has been since the day of Pentecost.

What a wonderful work could have been done for the vast company gathered in Battle Creek at the General Conference of 1901, if *the leaders of our work* had taken themselves in hand. But the work that all heaven was waiting to do as soon as men prepared the way, was not done; for *the leaders closed and bolted the door against the Spirit's entrance.* There was a stopping short of entire surrender to God. And hearts that might have been purified from all error were strengthened in wrong doing. The doors were barred against the heavenly current that would have swept away all evil. Men left their sins unconfessed. They built themselves up in wrong doing, and said to the Spirit of God, "Go Thy way for this time; when I have a more convenient season, I will call for Thee."—Letter to Dr. J. H. Kellogg, "Elmshaven," Sanitarium, Calif., August 5, 1902; italics supplied.

Again it must be asked: What do these words mean, do they actually mean what they say? Some may say, "They refer to Dr. Kellogg and his party." Surely they do; but it is very obvious that they mean much more than that. The exact phrases used are: "the men who had been bearing responsibilities," "the leaders of our work," "the leaders," "men." Humbly we would inquire of the Church: did the Latter Rain and the Loud Cry proceed satisfactorily after the 1901 Session?

This message was repeated almost word for word in a letter addressed to the General Conference Committee dated six days later. We all know that the profoundly tragic loss of Dr. Kellogg was to occur within a very few years. When he saw in the ministerial leadership of the church "a stopping short of entire surrender to God," surely his own heart, which "might have been purified from all error," was "strengthened in wrong doing. The doors were barred against the heavenly current that would have swept away all evil." This terribly serious letter clearly traces the cause that led to the effect. A failure to enter into denominational repentance by "the vast company gathered in Battle Creek at the General Conference of 1901" bore tragic fruit:

> The Lord calls for the close self-examination to be made now that was not made at the last General Conference, when He was waiting to be gracious. The present is our sowing time for eternity. We must reap the fruit of the evil seed we sow, unless we repent the sowing, and ask forgiveness for the mistakes we have made. Those

who, given opportunity to repent and reform, pass over the ground without humbling the heart before God, without putting away that which He reproves, will become hardened against the counsel of the Lord Jesus—"To the General Conference Committee and the Medical Missionary Board," Elmshaven, Sanitarium, Calif., August 11, 1902.

What was the "reaping" that came by and by?

We all know: the loss of Dr. Kellogg; the burning of the old and eventual separation from us of the new Battle Creek Sanitarium; the burning of the Review and Herald offices; and the removal of leadership headquarters from old Battle Creek. It was an overturning similar to the tragedy that befell Jerusalem and the Temple in the days of Jeremiah. This, we are told, was "victory."

Who knows the future before us now? No one. *But if the history of the past is worth anything*, we should tremble lest persistent denominational impenitence today become a "seedsowing" that will trigger a further sad series of events to include eventual separation of our chief medical institutions from our control, and another overturning of "Jerusalem."

If we insist on calling 1901 "victory" when the Lord's servant called it the "greatest sorrow" of her life, how can the Lord's call to repent ever get through to us? How can we understand "today" if we deny the facts of "yesterday"?

One is deeply impressed in reading Ellen G. White's testimonies that she carried a heart burden that few of her contemporaries understood or appreciated. Constantly she was aware of an ultimate spiritual preparation of heart that would make a people ready to finish the gospel work in all the world in that generation long ago, so the Lord could come. To confess that good sincere men failed to share that heart burden is not to disparage their memory in the least. If recognizing the truth can help us today to learn to share that heart burden, stating the facts can in no way be "an impeachment of the dead."

For example, consider the experience of the new General Conference President of 1901, as related frankly in *Movement of Destiny*:

> He [A. G. Daniells] told me with regret of his strange unawareness of the far-reaching principles and mighty potentials of Righteousness by Faith back in the earlier years of his ministry. ... He confided that in the long, intensive administration period of his general leadership—pressed by seemingly endless problems, and faced by beckoning challenges, as well as a succession of crises—these pressures came more and more to absorb his thoughts and energy. ...

As a result he neglected, he said, to keep up that essential intimacy of fellowship with God that he later sensed was so imperative for highest service. Absorption in dedicated activity for God has been allowed to crowd out that imperative personal spiritual advance that comes only through constant study of the deep things of God—along with much prayer and intercession. Such essentials came to be abbreviated in order to "keep the wheels turning," as he phrased it, in our "organizational machinery," for which he had the "leading responsibility." His Christian life had become a routine. ...

He told me that more and more he became absorbed in keeping the efficiency of the structural machinery of the Church at high level. ... As a result, Daniells came to rate men chiefly by their efficiency, their ability to get things done, their skill in the pulpit, and the leadership in the affairs of the Church—the *human* side. ... He had been much like the busy conductor of a transcontinental train, the captain of a great ship, or the manager of a giant business concern.—*Movement of Destiny*, pages 406, 407.

These were precisely the problems that wrung from Ellen G. White her appraisals of the true spiritual state of the post-1901 General Conference leadership.

The following is from a candid personal letter to a friend in whom she felt she could confide:

I do not now expect to attend the General Conference [of 1903]. I should not dare to go; for I am very much worn with the responsibilities that I have been carrying since the Fresno campmeeting. It is like this: when I stand before congregations of our people, I feel very intensely, because I understand the peril of those who as blind men have followed their own counsel. Were I to go to the Conference, I should be compelled to take positions that would cut some to the quick. It greatly hurts me to do this, and it is a long time before I recover from the strain that such an experience brings on me. ...

His [the Lord's] power was with me all the way through the last General Conference [1901], and had the men in responsibility felt one quarter of the burden that rested on me, there would have been heartfelt confession and repentance. A work would have been done by the Holy Spirit such as has never yet been seen in Battle Creek. Those who at that time heard my message, and refused to humble their hearts before God, are without excuse. ...

I know that matters in Battle Creek are in a most precarious condition. ...

The result of the last General Conference has been the greatest, the most terrible sorrow of my life. No change was made. The spirit that should have been brought into the whole work as the result of that meeting, was not brought in because men did not receive the testimonies of the Spirit of God. As they went to their several fields of labor, they did not walk in the light that the Lord had flashed upon their pathway, but carried into their work the wrong principles that had been prevailing in the work at Battle Creek.

The Lord has marked every movement made by the leading men in our institutions and conferences. It is a perilous thing to reject the light that God sends. ...

So today upon those who have had light and evidence, but who have refused to heed the Lord's warnings and entreaties, heaven's woe is pronounced. —Letter to Judge Jesse Arthur, "Elmshaven," Sanitarium, Calif., January 15, 1903.

WHAT ATTITUDE DID THE LORD'S MESSENGER TAKE?

The attitude of Ellen G. White towards the *result* of the 1901 Conference may be further clearly understood by referring to the published source in *Testimonies*, volume 8, pages 104 to 106. She wrote "To the Battle Creek Church" only ten days before she wrote the above letter to Judge Jesse Arthur. She says, "One day at noon I was writing of the work that might have been done at the last General Conference, if the men in positions of trust had followed the will and way of God. Those who have had great light have not walked in the light. The meeting was closed, and the break was not made. Men did not humble themselves before the Lord as they should have done, and the Holy Spirit was not imparted."—8T 104, St. Helena, Cal., Jan. 5, 1903. Her verdict of this 1901 Conference was almost in exactly the same tone as made for the 1888 session: "Now our meeting is drawing to a close, and not one confession has been made; there has not been a single break so as to let the Spirit of God in. Now I was saying, what was the use of our assembling here together and for our ministering brethren to come in if they are here only to shut out the Spirit of God from the people? "—*Through Crisis to Victory*, pages 290, 291. The tragic misconception of *Through Crisis to Victory* is the assumption that "what might have been" really happened. "What might have been" is portrayed in one of the most beautiful and poignant descriptions of a Spirit-filled meeting to be found in all the writings of the Spirit of Prophecy:

> We were assembled in the auditorium of the Tabernacle.. . . The meeting was marked by the presence of the Holy Spirit. The work

went deep, and some present were weeping aloud.

... One arose from his bowed position, and ... with great solemnity he repeated the message to the Laodicean church....

The speaker ... made heart-broken confessions, and then stepped up to several of the brethren, one after another, and extended his hand, asking forgiveness. Those to whom he spoke sprang to their feet, making confession and asking forgiveness, and they fell upon one another's necks, weeping. The spirit of confession spread through the entire congregation. It was a Pentecostal season.—8T 104, 105.

Absolutely beautiful! A meeting like that should certainly be called "Victory!" with the greatest enthusiasm. Such is the fruit of *genuine* "righteousness by faith." The only difficulty is that the "testimony" closes with these very sad words:

The words were spoken to me: *"This might have been."* ... I thought of where we might have been had thorough work been done at the last General Conference; and an agony of disappointment came over me as I realized that what I had witnessed was not a reality.—*Ibid.*, pages 105,106.

It is true that there are beautiful statements made either at the 1901 Conference or shortly afterwards about "the stately steppings of the Lord" there (R&H, Nov. 26, 1901), "He has given His Holy Spirit" (Letter 54, 1901), "God's angels have been walking up and down in this congregation" (1901 *Bulletin*, page 464), and some others. Surely the Lord blessed, and the re-organization effected was marvellous. Thank God for it. But Israel were likewise exceedingly well organized during their forty years of wandering in the wilderness, and Moses was on duty constantly to administer the work of God among them.

To be fair, we must consider the *result* of that 1901 Conference. The servant of the Lord wrote nearly two years later, "The *result* of the last General Conference has been the greatest, the most terrible sorrow of my life" (emphasis added). One would think that surely the author of *Through Crisis to Victory* read that letter, for he "studied thoroughly the records of the period as they are found in the voluminous files of the White Estate. Available to him were the Ellen G. White manuscript files" (Foreword, page 7). How then could he entitle his work, *Victory ... 1901?* The question is even more perplexing by the support *Movement of Destiny* gives the volume:

His is an accurate and dependable portrayal of that special period— 1888 to 1901. Fortunately his book had the advantage of painstaking checking and editing by the White Publications staff—a definite aid and safeguard.—Page 612.

This book assumes Mrs. White's 1901 hopes were fulfilled. Recognizing that the administration problems of the 1890s were a direct outgrowth of 1888 unbelief, she hopefully said, "Many who have been more or less out of line since the Minneapolis meeting will be brought into line." (*General Conference Bulletin*, 1901, page 205.) Precisely because this bright hope for reversal of the 1888 unbelief was disappointed, she later said the "result" of this Conference was "the greatest, the most terrible sorrow of my life. No change was made." Should not and will not the Church expect a correction to be made to the world field?

In pondering the above letter to Judge Jesse Arthur, one might be perplexed about isolated one-sentence excerpts quoted frequently that speak of the prophet's apparent satisfaction in the progress the Church was making. We have "as Bible Christians ever been on gaining ground" (2 SM 396-397); "for the past fifty years ... the presence of the Spirit of God [has been] with us as a people (2SM 397); and "I can say, See what the Lord hath wrought" (R&H, November 17, 1910). But one or two-sentence statements should be read in larger context. For example, the last one is significant. The very next sentence adds, "We need not feel sadness, except as we see a failure on the part of God's people to follow their Leader step by step." Never does Ellen G. White deny the necessity for repentance on our part as a people!

And there are two aspects of "progress:" one, that of building an ever larger and more powerful church organization, increasing in numbers, wealth, and prestige, and that can stand for hundreds of years as have the great Protestant churches; and secondly, the true progress of making a people ready for the coming of the Lord through a wholehearted acceptance of what Ellen G. White called "the message of Christ's righteousness," a message to prepare the harvest grain for the heavenly sickle.

THE HONOR AND VINDICATION OF CHRIST IS INVOLVED IN THIS!

There is clear evidence that this was the "burden" that the Lord's servant bore on her heart in a special way from 1888 onwards to her death. Had her brethren "felt one quarter of the burden that rested on me, ... a work would have been done by the Holy Spirit such as has never yet been seen in Battle Creek," she declared.

There is a little-known statement that discloses how the Lord Jesus Himself felt about the post-1901 spiritual state of the ministry and the church:

> God says to His people, "I have somewhat against thee, because thou has left thy first love ..."
>
> Leaving the first love is represented as a spiritual fall. Many have fallen thus. In every church in our land, there is needed confessions, repentance, and reconversion. The disappointment of Christ is beyond description. ... Christ is humiliated in His people. ...
>
> My brethren and sisters, humble your hearts before the Lord. ... I cannot fail to see that the light which God has given to me is not favorable to our ministers or our churches. ... The message to the Laodicean church reveals our condition as a people.—*Review and Herald*, December 15, 1904.

Sixteen years after 1888, can the condition portrayed here by the servant of the Lord be considered in any way as an "awakening from Laodicean self-satisfaction and self-reliance, a renewal brought about through the growing acceptance of the message of Righteousness by Faith"? With love and deep respect the question must be asked, Is "the light" of the full truth "favorable" to us today?

She never forgot the deep meaning of the "message of Christ's righteousness." As late as 1906 she still yearned to witness its triumph:

> Dear Brethren Washburn, Prescott, Daniells, and Concord:
>
> ... Christ came, and in the likeness of man wrought out before the world a perfect character, that the world may be without excuse.. . .
>
> Had our churches heeded the words of the Lord's messenger, given them by pen and voice, had they taken their position as true believers, we should have seen a most wonderful ingathering, which would have convinced the world that we have the truth. The law of God would have been magnified. And the Sunday law, that leading men are trying to bring in, could have had but little influence. But hindrances in the very midst of us have worked counter to the purpose of God. My heart is almost broken as I think of what the Lord has opened to me in regard to what might have been, but is not.—Letter W-58, 1906, Sanitarium, Calif.

In bringing to a close this presentation of Ellen G. White testimony, we want to make clear that we have never doubted the Lord's special watchcare and blessing over His true Church, which we believe is the Seventh-day Adventist Church. He will keep step with us in all our wanderings. We have never believed that He has cast off His Church! We understand that the original Greek of the message to the "angel of the church of the Laodiceans" does not say that Christ has actually spewed His people out of His "mouth" but only that He is "about to" do so because of the terrible nausea He feels on account of our "lukewarm" condition. The point of our manuscript of twenty-two years ago was that it is not fair to Him for us to perpetuate the condition that occasioned the Lord's servant to write: "Christ is humiliated in His people."

That is the point of this present "Confession." When will we permit Him to work that glorious "what might have been" in the finishing of His work in our own hearts?

What can possibly arouse us to see this in the light in which the heavenly universe view it? The authors firmly take their stand with the following statement made at the 1893 Session by A. T. Jones:

> We stand pledged to the Lord and before the world: that we depend upon God; that He loves His people; that He manifests Himself in behalf of those whose hearts are toward Him. Brethren, there is that fearful word also that touches that very thought, that came to us from Australia [by Ellen G. White]. It is in the testimony entitled, "The Crisis Imminent." What does that say? —"Something great and decisive is to take place, and that right early. If any delay, the character of God and His throne will be compromised." Brethren, by our careless, indifferent attitude, we are putting God's throne into jeopardy. Why cannot He work? God is ready. Are not God's workmen ready? But if there is any delay, "the character of God and His throne is jeopardized." Is it possible that we are about to risk the honor of God's throne? Brethren, for the Lord's sake, and for His throne's sake, let us get out of the way.—*General Conference Bulletin*, 1893, pages 73, 74.

WHAT CAN WE SAY?

After reading these statements from the testimonies of Ellen G. White, one can begin to sense something of the problem faced by the authors of *1888 Re-examined*. On the one hand, *Movement of Destiny*, with General Conference endorsement, calls from us "an explicit confession" to the Church apologizing for saying that there was a leadership rejection of the very message which was intended by the Lord to prepare a people for His coming eighty years ago. On the other hand, our conscience is bound by the clear testimony of the Spirit of Prophecy.

Common sense forces the conclusion that if "we" had accepted the 1888 message for what it truly was, the "beginning" of the Latter Rain and Loud Cry, we would not be in this world today. The Church would not be faced with an ever-expanding world task as yet unfinished.

Ellen G. White does not contradict her own testimony. No word has been found in her published works nor will such in the future be found in any of her unpublished writings that contradicts the plain import of the statements cited in this paper. Such does not exist. The authors of *Through Crisis to Victory*, and *Movement of Destiny* have thoroughly combed the collection of unpublished writings in the Vault, and have found nothing. This is now obvious from reading their exhaustive treatises on the subject.

At the same time both the authors of *Movement of Destiny* and *Through Crisis to Victory* affirm their honesty and objectivity. The author of the former says of his own work:

> There is nothing like it in all our annals—or any other annals for that matter. ... There is no hiding of facts, no build-up of fanciful fictions—just the simple truth. ... It neither shields nor slants, but tells the facts as they are. ... Faithfully factual. ... The inside story ... is now set forth in fulness for the first time. ... Forthrightly told. ... Provides the inner meaning behind the outward facts. ... An expedition in quest of all the facts. ... The bounden obligation to report it to the Church ... has been my constant burden. ... A faithful fuller history. ... Extraordinary care has been taken to provide an accurate, faithful, balanced presentation of the Gift [the Spirit of Prophecy].—*The Fascinating Story of Movement of Destiny*, pages 3-11.

We as authors, are conscience bound by what is evident to us in the abundant Spirit of Prophecy testimony. This testimony declares that the post-1888 and post-1901 Church leadership did not truly appreciate and accept the gracious message that should have finished the work in their generation. The only possible conclusion is to recognize that the Lord calls for denominational repentance and humbling of heart today. Our position as authors is portrayed as follows:

> PERSISTENCE OF CHARGES SHEER STUBBORNNESS.— ... One can only come to the conclusion that persistent clinging to such a charge is sheer stubbornness, based on a personal stance that has been taken and that must be maintained irrespective of the actual evidence and the testimony of facts that persuade all others.—*Movement of Destiny*, page 686.

We earnestly inquire, "Where is the Ellen G. White 'testimony' that persuades 'all others'?" Any "testimony" that contradicts Ellen G. White's own clear words is a fiction. As authors we do not want to be guilty of "sheer stubbornness." We choose to be loyal to Christ and His truth. The publication of *Movement of Destiny* has placed before us, a dilemma completely unprecedented in Seventh-day Adventist history.

A SOLUTION MUST BE FOUND

Two problems cry for an answer and a solution:

1. Did "we" truly reject the Lord's gracious message eighty years ago? Have "we" learned our lesson or is our general heart-attitude the same today as it was then? *In other words, does the Lord Himself call for a repentance?*

2. Have we truly recovered the essentials of the 1888 message today? Is that which we are preaching now as "righteousness by faith," as it gets through to the people, truly an accurate and effective modern presentation of the fundamental truths of 1888? Or could it be that we have unwittingly substituted instead the concepts of the popular Evangelical and Protestant churches? *If the latter is true, then our boasted "riches" of understanding and preaching righteousness by faith are in vain.*

Actually, answering the first problem will become unnecessary if we can discover the answer to the second problem. This is the real issue! The popular assumption is that we do understand "righteousness by faith," because that phrase constantly abounds on our tongues and appears in our contemporary literature. If we *talk* about it so much surely we must *have* it!

Ellen G. White's phrase of April 1, 1901 is very impressive, "professedly accepting it" but "making no change." The mere use of terminology does not mean the clear presence of the truth of the message. The authors insist that the fundamental concepts and dominant features of the genuine 1888 message are not understood by our people today. This is not because our laity are slow to appreciate them, but because they are *in general* not being presented today, with but few exceptions. The authors have maintained for two decades that a "hidden hunger" exists, and that we as a church are in reality undernourished while we exhibit symptoms of spiritual flabbiness and "overweight." They have asserted this is due to the fact that Satan has cleverly deceived us into thinking we are "rich and increased with goods" in our assumed understanding of "righteousness by faith" when what we really have is closer to the modern counterfeit of righteousness by faith as taught by "Babylon." Our message should be, "Babylon is fallen." The fact remains that in respect to the very "gospel" itself—"righteousness by faith," most of us are at a loss to distinguish between the concepts as taught by the popular churches and as taught by us. Constantly we are confronted by people who have been through our various Bible Courses who say, "We see no difference between what Adventists teach and what our church teaches except the Sabbath and a few 'doctrines.'"

If that is true, then indeed we as a people have no real contribution to make beyond the message of the other churches except legalism. The popular churches teach the "gospel," and all we have to add is the "law." But surely this cannot be true! The first angel's message is "the everlasting *gospel*." Has the Lord indeed entrusted the proclamation of *that* message to the popular Evangelical churches? Are we merely "me-too's"? Have we no understanding of the very "everlasting gospel" itself that is unique? Yes, we must, indeed, *we do!* And it is time that we understand it thoroughly so that we can give it to the world clearly.

Bear in mind that the gospel is genuine "righteousness by faith." Only that can produce the blessed "what might have been" fruits so long delayed. Can someone clearly tell the difference between the basic idea of the "gospel" as taught by the popular Evangelical revivalists of today and what *we* think is the "gospel"? The authors have found precious few of our ministers or laity who can accept this challenge. We believe that this inability is due directly to a widespread ignorance of what the 1888 message was.

This idea, that we come away from the table with "hidden hunger," has been shocking to contemplate. It has aroused a storm of protest. Some are so certain that "all is well" that they have wished to see the authors silenced for all time without the church ever being permitted to see or have a chance to consider firsthand the evidence put forth. Some who may not purpose to silence them ask in pained shock, "How could we misunderstand 'righteousness by faith' when we have such an abundance of Spirit of Prophecy writings available to study?"

The answer to this question is found by pointing to the Jewish nation who misunderstood and rejected their Messiah when they had the Old Testament in its fulness and read from it every Sabbath. They read and listened with what Paul called a "vail ... upon their heart." 2 Cor. 3:15. We too, have our *own* history. "We have nothing to fear for the future except as we shall forget the way the Lord has led us in the past." In old Battle Creek in the 1890s, our dear brethren had a great abundance of Spirit of Prophecy material before them constantly, plus Ellen G. White's living presence.

Obviously the physical possession of Ellen G. White books today does not necessarily mean a clear grasp of truth any more than having her personal presence and listening to her words eighty years ago. A "vailed" reading does not solve the problem.

A re-publication of the clear teaching of the 1888 messengers themselves would automatically reveal the great contrast between what we popularly assume is the gospel and what Ellen G. White said was "a most precious message" from the Lord. A trial presentation of this message before hundreds of our lay members in 1971 has substantiated this as a fact. The overwhelming written testimony was that the original 1888 message was refreshingly different than standard fare today. Ideas and concepts abound in the original sources that almost never find expression in our literature or pulpits today.

CAN SOMETHING BE DONE?

There is a solution to this problem and it is so simple that it cannot be misunderstood: We need a revival of the genuine message of righteousness by faith as the Lord sent it to us; and the 1888 message is a good place to begin.

1. If, as it is widely affirmed, we as a people have enjoyed a genuine and thorough revival of the 1888 message since the 1920s, why hasn't the work of God been finished in our time? The books, *Movement of Destiny*, *Through Crisis to Victory*, *The Faith That Saves*, and *By Faith Alone*, all clearly proclaim that in the 1920s and in our present decades "righteousness by faith" has enjoyed virtual "unanimity" of acceptance. "I have never heard a worker or a laymember in America, Europe, or anywhere else—express opposition to the message of righteousness by faith."—*Through Crisis to Victory*, page 232. This claim of virtual "unanimity" of acceptance of "righteousness by faith" since the 1920s is in contrast to the doubtful reception of eighty years ago. Surely this more recent acceptance, if true, ought to accomplish in *forty* years what Ellen G. White said the acceptance of the 1888 message would have accomplished in *four* years! See 1893 *General Conference Bulletin*, page 419.

SOMETHING IS NOT RIGHT!

If the "medicine" one takes for forty years obviously fails to cure the "disease," is it not wisdom to at least take a second look to enquire if it is potent medicine? This the authors appealed for twenty-two years ago!

2. Some say "As a church we understand righteousness by faith and we preach it clearly; our problem is simply that we don't live it as we should."

Think this through carefully. We all agree that "righteousness" is by "faith." Obviously then, if one has "faith," he will certainly have "righteousness" manifest in his life. He will live it. If this is not true, then the term is nothing but semantic nonsense. To Seventh-day Adventists "righteousness by faith" is clearly a preparation of character for the coming of the Lord. Otherwise, "what do we more than others?"

The Lord's servant has recognized this clearly. Speaking of the 1888 message, she said, "The enemy of man and God is not willing that this truth should be fully presented: for he knows that if the people receive it fully, his power will be broken."—R&H, September 3, 1889.

Is the enemy's power "broken" in our lives as a church? When his power is truly "broken," will not the Lord's people be ready for His coming? And if we are not *ready*, and have not been for eighty years, either we do not fully understand and therefore do not receive the truth of righteousness by faith, or else the Lord is to blame for the long delay in His return. If we understand it but do not "receive it fully," then we are most truly rejecting it This is a very dangerous thing to do. If to some extent we truly understand and receive "this truth," which is not a doctrine, but rather "light," to that extent Satan's power over us is broken. But above all, as Seventh-day Adventists we are not merely to get a people ready to *die*; we are to prepare a people to live, ready for *translation!* If this is not true, no one knows how many more decades must elapse before the world's burden of sorrow and pain can be lifted.

We "confess" that "righteousness by faith" is what it says—right living by faith. *Therefore it is impossible truly to understand it and preach it dearly without living it truly!*

True New Testament "faith" is very close to repentance and contrition. It is what the early church experienced. When we call for denominational repentance, we are really calling for a true experience of "faith" in contrast to the counterfeit so popular today. The "final atonement" is in this call.

3. What to do? (a) Check what were the essential and unique truths of the inspired 1888 message for they are clearly on record, says *Movement of Destiny*, pages 189, 200, 201; (b) Compare these essentials with "righteousness by faith" as generally taught by me popular churches of today; (c) Then contrast the 1888 message with *our* contemporary presentations of "righteousness by faith." The authors have maintained for two decades that the difference between (a) and (c) is so striking as to be astonishing. We have been asleep as a people! In truth, we need the message today as much as our brethren needed it in 1888.

4. The fact that *Movement of Destiny* has been published now is proof positive of the all-important place that the 1888 General Conference Session holds in the history of this denomination, no matter what one believes regarding the acceptance or rejection of the message by "few," "some," or "many." Parallel with this must be the recognition that *1888 Re-examined* after twenty years of official censure has by its very content come to a place of supplying at least partial answers to current problems the church faces. The wide acceptance of this latter document and the weight of the evidence it presents must surely account for the heavy thrust and indictment made against it by *Movement of Destiny*. It is self-evident that the basic idea of one or the other of these treatises is wrong. *Factually* the matter could be settled once and for all by the publication, in chronological order without comment, of all that the Lord had told His people about this era as found in the Spirit of Prophecy. *Spiritually* the matter can be settled only at such time as God's people and in particular the leadership, choose to accept all that He has said irrespective of any rationalization man may offer or how much his pride may be humbled.

The solemn call to denominational repentance is firmly rejected by *Movement of Destiny* in the following words:

> Recurrent harpers [and] ... echoers still persist, maintaining that the leadership of the Movement, at that time [1888 and post-1888] "rejected" the message of Righteousness by Faith, and thereby incurred the continuing disfavor of God.
>
> And along with that assumption and assertion goes a contention that until and unless the *Movement as a whole today*—nearly eighty years later—repents as a body in sackcloth and ashes for the sins of the "some" who, back at that fateful time, did definitely reject the Minneapolis Message at and following 1888, the smile and benediction of God will never rest upon the Advent people and Movement, and its message will never be consummated under present conditions.
>
> In other words, such maintain that the Loud Cry and Latter Rain will never be visited upon us until that retroactive penitence requirement is met through some official acknowledgement and action. That is surely a most sobering thought—if true. On this point let us seek out the facts and find the truth concerning such retrospective repentance.
>
> ... If not true, it constitutes an unjustifiable woe uttered against the Church as a whole today, affirmed some eight decades after the acts of 1888.—Pages 357, 358.
>
> Is there such a thing as present-day denomination-wide guilt, because of the wrong attitude of the "some" who rejected the Righteousness

by Faith message at and following 1888, which must be atoned for by some all-inclusive "corporate" confession of the denomination as a whole before we can receive the unstinted blessing of God? ...

... God will not hold guiltless those who seek to impugn the men in leadership who personally accepted the message and sought to lead His people forward in harmony therewith.

Away then, with such charges.—Pages 445, 451.

The authors are sure that the author of Movement of Destiny did not intend to distort their position on "corporate" and "denominational repentance." It seems obvious that he did not understand it. But it is very clear that once and for all he firmly rejects and even spurns the idea of denominational repentance for the sin of rejecting the beginning of the Latter Rain and Loud Cry. He insists that the post-1888 leadership accepted it. This rejection of the call to denominational repentance is intrinsically endorsed by "some sixty of our ablest scholars—specialists in denominational history and Adventist theology ... experts in the Spirit of Prophecy, ... key Bible teachers, editors, mass communications men, scientists, physicians ... and veteran leaders ... verifiers and copy editors. ... Doubtless no volume in our history has ever had such magnificent prepublication support."—Movement of Destiny, page 8.

It follows that the demand on the authors to make "an explicit confession ... due the Church" is likewise endorsed by the "magnificent prepublication support" of this volume. We dare not refuse to "confess." All that the authors have ever said regarding the need for denominational repentance as necessary to the honor and vindication of Christ has been said in love for our brethren and in loyalty to church organization. We are a part of that organization and therefore cannot in any way disassociate ourselves from such needs and weaknesses as may be in the "body."

We therefore stand before the Church with the firm conviction that the Spirit of Prophecy counsel and writings clearly portray the facts of our history, and we are conscience-bound to accept this as a "Thus saith the Lord! " and so, we accordingly make—

OUR "CONFESSION"

1. *We confess the truth of our Lord's words*: "Because thou sayest, I am rich, and increased with goods, and have need of nothing [the authors acknowledge that this appeal is specifically directed to the ministry and the leadership of the Laodicean church] ; and knowest not that thou art wretched, and miserable, and poor, and blind, and naked."

Revelation 3:17. We believe that our Lord here refers primarily to "our" pride in our understanding of the gospel, "our" vaunted assumption that "we" "understand" "righteousness by faith." An example in point is the conclusion of the book *Through Crisis to Victory* which almost wholly exonerates *us as ministers* today and lays the blame for the unfinished task upon the laity:

> Anyone who takes the time to examine Seventh-day Adventist books, papers, pamphlets, and tracts will discover that this glorious truth has been printed time and time again. ...
>
> Representative books by Seventh-day Adventist authors that have issued from denominational presses in North America—not to mention those published in other lands—and that have dealt with the subject of righteousness by faith, are many. ...
>
> Through the years since 1901 and before, Seventh-day Adventists have published numerous tracts on righteousness by faith, and from time to time this theme has been covered in Sabbath school lessons. The various phases of salvation through faith in Christ have been taught with power and clarity over the radio for a number of years and more recently on television. This subject has been made prominent in different courses of Bible correspondence lessons. Adventist pastors and evangelists have announced this vital truth from church pulpits and public platforms, with hearts aflame with love for Christ. And through the monthly journal, The Ministry, Seventh-day Adventist preachers and writers have constantly been urged to make Jesus Christ and His righteousness as the Saviour, the center of all their teaching. ...
>
> Many Seventh-day Adventists still seem ignorant of this all-important doctrine. Much of this lack of awareness results from their failure to read Adventist books and periodicals presenting the gospel in clear, forceful language. ...
>
> We fear that to many *church members* the message of righteousness by faith has become a dry theory instead of a living reality in *their* daily experience.
>
> *They* have neglected the light that God in His love and mercy has caused to shine upon them. *They* have failed to exchange the worthless garments of *their own* self-righteousness for the spotless robe of Christ's righteousness. In the sight of God *their* poor souls are naked and destitute. Unless *they* heed the counsel of the True Witness to buy of Him the white raiment, that the shame of *their* nakedness may not appear, *they* will soon be rejected by their Lord.—Pages 233-239, italics supplied.

Yes, the ministry are "rich, and increased with goods, and have need of nothing." Yet it can be shown clearly that the fundamental concepts of the 1888 message are largely absent from most of this teaching with the exception of the Ellen G. White publications! What is commonly understood to be "righteousness by faith" is the popular Protestant, Evangelical view, and it is assumed that if we tack onto *their* understanding of "righteousness by faith" our own "peculiar doctrines," lo, we have Adventism.

The above quotation seeks to find in the laity some "scapegoat" to account for the long delay in the finishing of the church's gospel commission. The Spirit of Prophecy clearly upholds the principle of "like priest, like people:" "The members of our churches are not incorrigible; the fault is not so much to be charged upon them as upon their teachers. Their ministers do not feed them."—*Special Testimonies*, No. 10, November, 1890.

2. *We confess a brighter hope than this despairing view affords.* If we as leaders are right and yet the church members will not follow the light, where is there any hope that the church will ever get ready for the coming of the Lord—even if we wait another eighty years? We believe the full truth and the understanding of the tragic failures of our past denominational history give the brightest hope for a speedy finishing of the work in glorious victory in our generation. Why? Because knowing the full truth will clear our minds and the minds of our membership and the minds of our youth of all lingering doubt that *perhaps the Lord Himself has delayed His coming* and is unresponsive to our prayers. If our prayers are not yet answered, we can either doubt the Lord's faithfulness, which is pure despair; or else recognize our *own* unfaithfulness and confess it, which is a positive solution. If the Lord is unfaithful there is nothing that can be done about it. If *we* are, surely repentance will enable us to do something about that!

3. *We confess that we understand our Lord's words in Revelation 3:19 to be a clear call to denominational repentance:* "Be zealous therefore, and repent."

(a) He addresses the message to "the *angel* of the church of the Laodiceans." Verse 14. "The angels of the seven churches" are "the seven stars" in Christ's "right hand." Verses 16, 20. "God's ministers are symbolized by the seven stars."—GW 13. They are "the teachers in the church—those entrusted by God with weighty responsibilities," especially "those in the offices that God has appointed for the leadership of His people." (Compare AA 164, 586.) Therefore Christ's call to "repent" is directed primarily to the leadership of His Church.

(b) What should we repent of? Our spiritual pride and self-sufficiency! Revelation 3:17. We do not sense our need of "the message of Christ's righteousness." We assume that we *have* the message and therefore understand it. We commend ourselves for faithfully proclaiming it to the world, especially in recent decades. Yet in fact we honestly do not know our destitution! We are sincere in supposing that we understand "righteousness by faith" as presented in the 1888 message when we have lost or never understood the fundamental dominant feature that gave that message its vital power. What we proudly assume is "righteousness by faith" as we practically understand it consists of themes and concepts borrowed either from the great Reformers of the sixteenth century or from modern Evangelicals. In a similar way the Jews "had" the Sabbath for millenniums but it is obvious from the words of our Lord that they did not understand it, or appreciate its true significance or in any way truly "keep" it. Our spiritual ignorance parallels theirs. "Thou knowest not ..." is an accurate depiction of *our* condition generally. Jesus says it!

(c) To recognize in our denominational history an echo of Christ's call to the "angel" or leadership of the church to "repent" is not in any way disloyalty or subversion, although it has often been so interpreted by offended individuals. For millenniums, offense has been taken at calls to repent. A typical example is that of the "priests and the prophets" who accused Jeremiah to "the princes and to all the people, saying. This man is worthy to die; for he hath prophesied against this city." Jeremiah 26:11. Yet from our modern perspective it is clear that Jeremiah was in reality "prophesying" *for* the commonweal of the "city."

We "confess" that recognizing in our history a clear call to "repent" is for the good of modern Israel as well as for the vindication of our Lord. There is therefore no need of apologizing for proclaiming His call as found in His Word and as illustrated in our history. "As many as I love," He says, "I rebuke and chasten." Such "chastening" does not require the personal services of another living prophet to take the place of Ellen G. White. All that is required is to know the full, unvarnished, whole truth of our denominational history. Honest hearts will immediately respond.

(d) Such repentance will in no way weaken the authority or lesson the respect due to official church leadership. We "confess" with insistence that leadership in denominational repentance will immediately increase the genuine respect the world-church will have for the General Conference.

4. *We confess that a repentance on the part of this generation for the failures of a past generation is highly in order.*

(a) *It is biblical.* "If they shall confess their iniquity, and the iniquity of their fathers, with their trespass which they trespassed against Me, and that also they have walked contrary unto Me; and that I also have walked contrary to them ..." Leviticus 26:40, 41. King Josiah accepted what Moses said, recognized that the sins of his "fathers" were in reality *is* sins, and confessed: "Great is the wrath of the Lord that is kindled against us, because *our fathers* have not hearkened unto the words of this book." 2 Kings 22:13. Nehemiah also recognized the same principle of corporate identity with the previous generations: "Both I and my father's house have sinned." Nehemiah 1:6. There are many Old Testament examples. (See Appendix A for a fuller treatment of this subject.)

If the Lord held Israel in Ezekiel's day responsible for the sins of *her* "youth" (see Ezekiel 16, the whole of the chapter), how can "we" disclaim responsibility for the sins of "our" youth? "Denominational repentance" is simply what the Lord calls for throughout His Word. The "final atonement" we have been talking about for so long comes simply from recognizing the full truth of "our" position before the Lord and the watching universe. Those who will humble their hearts in honest recognition of the truth are the "woman" who will in contrition prepare to be the Lamb's "wife."

(b) *Christ appealed to the Jewish nation of His day for a denominational repentance.* "From that time began Jesus to preach, and to say, Repent: for the kingdom of heaven is at hand." Matthew 4:17. He upbraided "the cities wherein most of His mighty works were done, because they repented not." Matthew 11:20. "These three years I come seeking fruit on this fig tree, and find none." Luke 13:6-9. Jesus' last public discourse was a final appeal to the Jewish leadership at Jerusalem to repent, and a heart-broken lament for their refusal to do so (Matthew 23:13-27).

(c) *Jesus appealed to the repentance of Nineveh as a "model" for the Jewish leaders to follow in denominational repentance.* "The men of Nineveh shall rise up in the judgment with this generation, and shall condemn it: for they repented." Luke 11:29-32. This "model" repentance is an example for us to follow, too: "The people of Nineveh believed God ... from the greatest of them to the least of them. For word came unto the king of Nineveh, and he arose from his throne, and he laid his robe from him ... and caused it to be proclaimed and published through Nineveh by the decree of the king and his nobles." Jonah 3:3-7. One might say that Nineveh's repentance was led by their "General Conference Committee."

(d) *Jesus taught the principle of solidarity of His Jewish generation with their ancestors in their guilt:* "Woe unto you ... that upon you may come all the righteous blood shed upon the earth, from the blood of righteous Abel unto the blood of Zacharias son of Barachias, whom ye slew between the temple and the altar. Verily I say unto you, All these things shall come upon this generation." Matthew 23:29-36. (This Zacharias was murdered about 856 BC.) The principle here expressed in no way contradicts Ezekiel's dictum that guilt is not genetically or legally inherited by the children (Ezekiel 18:20), but Jesus was expressing the principle of *corporate* guilt, not *inherited* guilt. "Whom *ye* slew," He said, although the murdered man lived long before any of His hearers were born; and He charged upon them the guilt even of Abel's blood. Why this corporate guilt? Because His hearers were actually guilty of Cain's sin and the sin of Zacharias' murderers. This they soon demonstrated in the murder of the Son of God. Ezra recognized the same principle of corporate guilt: "Since the days of our fathers have we been in a great trespass unto this day; and for *our* iniquities have we, our kings, and our priests, been delivered into the hand of the kings of the lands." Ezra 9:7. They were "one body" in guilt.

(e) *The writings of Ellen G. White recognize the Bible principle of corporate and denominational guilt, and the need for corporate and denominational repentance.* For example, the sin of Calvary is a sin for which we are *all* alike guilty, even though the sin of crucifying Christ took place nearly two thousand years before any of us were born. We can never be saved unless we individually participate in a corporate repentance for this sin of sins:

> Let us remember that we are still in a world where Jesus, the Son of God, was rejected and crucified, where the guilt of despising Christ and preferring a robber rather than the spotless Lamb of God still rests. Unless we individually repent toward God because of transgression of His law, and exercise faith toward our Lord Jesus Christ, whom the world has rejected, we shall lie under the full condemnation that the action of choosing Barabbas instead of Christ merited. The whole world stands charged today with the deliberate rejection and murder of the Son of God. The word bears record that Jews and Gentiles, kings, governors, ministers, priests, and people—all classes and sects who reveal the same spirit of envy, hatred, prejudice, and unbelief manifested by those who put to death the Son of God—would act the same part, were the opportunity granted, as did the Jews and people of the time of Christ. They would be partakers of the same spirit that demanded the death of the Son of God.—TM 38.

God's law reaches the feelings and motives, as well as the outward acts. It reveals the secrets of the heart, flashing light upon things before buried in darkness. God knows every thought, every purpose, every plan, every motive. The books of heaven record the sins that would have been committed had there been opportunity.—ST, July 31, 1901; 5BC 1085.

That prayer of Christ for His enemies ["Father, forgive them; for they know not what they do"] embraced the world. It took in every sinner that had lived or should live, from the beginning of the world to the end of time. Upon all rests the guilt of crucifying the Son of God.—DA 745.

What is "corporate repentance"? It is repenting of sin which we may not have actually done, but which we would have committed had we had the opportunity or been under sufficient pressure. Already "the books of heaven record" these sins against our names. "God's law reaches the feelings and motives." Therefore we are already guilty of these sins that we would commit if we had the opportunity. Corporate repentance is recognizing this truth that as part of the "body" we share in the sins of the "body."

Two examples of such repentance are obvious:

(i) *Repentance for the sin of crucifying Christ*. Although we weren't even born when He was crucified, Inspiration says that aside from specific repentance for this sin, "we shall be under the full condemnation that the action of choosing Barabbas instead of Christ merited" (TM 38). This is what Paul meant when he said that "what things soever the law saith, it saith to them who are under the law: that every mouth may be stopped, and *all the world* may become guilty before God." Romans 3:19. In its fullest sense, "transgression of His law" is the murder of the Son of God. If we are sinners at all, it is *that* sin of which we are potentially guilty.

Therefore repentance for *sin*, not just for *acts* of sin, is essential. This is the very essence of New Testament "righteousness by faith." When the apostles preached this mighty truth, this was its meaning. They charged upon the people their guilt in crucifying Christ, both Jews and Gentiles. All saw it. "Faith" was deep heart-sorrow for participation in the murder of the Messiah, and a heart-appreciation of His forgiving love. It is no wonder that Paul's doctrine of "righteousness by faith" turned the world upside down! And it is no wonder ours is so tame—we lack the full truth. When Paul brought home to his hearers their guilt, even though they themselves may not have been physically present at Calvary, it was corporate repentance that they were experiencing.

(ii) *Repentance for the sin of rejecting the "beginning of the Latter Rain" at and after 1888.* This has delayed the coming of Christ for many decades. This sin also took place long before we were even born; but unless we had fully experienced the kind of corporate repentance mentioned above, we would have done the same thing in 1888 that our brethren did, had we been there. We are really no better than they. Corporate repentance is realizing that *their* sin is *our* sin. It is putting ourselves in their place and realizing how the books of heaven faithfully record that we are just as guilty as they. Our human nature is the same as theirs was. Only by this experience can the terrible stranglehold of Laodicean pride be broken forever!

The sin of Calvary and the sin of 1888 are both revelations of the deep sinfulness of our own hearts. We all partake of a common humanity, and this sin of sins is our basic human common-denominator. Corporate repentance is individually repenting as though what *apparently* is the sin of others were really our own (as it is!).

What then is "denominational repentance"? It is this glorious individual experience of corporate repentance and true faith permeating the entire denomination from the top to the bottom. It is a repentance exactly like that of Nineveh of old, which began at the king's palace and extended throughout the empire. It is recognizing our responsibility *as a people* that we have delayed the coming of the Lord all these many decades. What sufferings this has caused unnecessarily only these same "books of heaven" can record. We know that two World Wars are included, and how many others and how much more only Heaven knows. Denominational repentance is recognizing and acknowledging our true position as we stand "miserable" and "naked" before the watching eyes of the heavenly universe. It is not an experience legislated by committees and promoted by departments amidst organizational fanfare. Denominational repentance will be individual corporate repentance permeating the denomination, starting with the General Conference.* The need is expressed as follows:

---

* This principle may be studied further by reference to additional Spirit of Prophecy writings. The 1888 sin of rejection of the message was a specific manifestation of the same sin that led the Jews to reject Christ. This is stated many times. For some examples, see TM 96, 97; FE 472; *Review and Herald*, May 27, 1890; April 11, 1893; etc. The barren fig-tree represents not a mere mass of individual unrepentant Jews, but the corporate body of the nation which rejected Christ (DA 582; COL 308; AA 78, 79). [continued ...]

Many have accepted the theory of the truth, who have had no true conversion. I know whereof I speak. There are few who feel true sorrow for sin; who have deep, pungent convictions of the depravity of the unregenerate nature. The heart of stone is not exchanged for a heart of flesh. Few are willing to fall upon the Rock, and be broken.

No matter who you are, or what your life has been, you can be saved only in God's appointed way. You must repent; you must fall helpless on the Rock, Christ Jesus.—5T 218.

We are told in *Movement of Destiny* that this principle of corporate and denominational repentance is wrong, citing "a paralleling case" as evidence. Here is the statement in full context as presented in *Movement of Destiny*:

> There is yet another basic principle involved in this matter of confession that must never be forgotten. It is the fundamental truth that those of us who live today are not accountable for the sins of our spiritual ancestors. They themselves must bear that blame. Mrs. White sets forth this principle in a paralleling case:
>
> "Those who live in this day are not accountable for the deeds of those who crucified the Son of God." (E.G.W., R&H, April 11, 1893, p. 226.)
>
> It is the actual "soul that sinneth" who "shall die" (Eze. 18:4, 20) for *his own* sin—if he does not repent. And, in harmony with this obviously just principle, there is not a line on record in all the writings of the Spirit of Prophecy calling upon the Church—the present General Conference leadership and denominational body as a whole, of today—to confess the sins of the individuals comprising

---

[... continued] Their corporate sin was accomplished through the action of their "religious leaders," which bound the nation to corporate ruin (COL 305). Only a national repentance could therefore have saved the Jewish nation from the impending ruin which their corporate sin invoked upon them (AA 247). As already noted, Ellen G. White clearly recognized that the 1888 guilt was incurred by "the brethren," "the heart of the work," "our brethren," etc., generic terms denoting far more than a scattered few individuals. The rejectors bound the denominational leadership to "communicating" "the disease at the heart of the work which poisons the blood" "until it has tainted and corrupted the whole" and "imbued" even foreign workers "with the spiritual leprosy of Battle Creek" (Letters, August 27, 1896; May 31, 1896). The process by which this guilt operated was as real as that by which the Sanhedrin led the Jewish nation to reject Christ (TM 64-77; *Review and Herald*, March 18, 1890; MS. 13, 1889; *Through Crisis to Victory*, page 292).

the "some" who sinned back there at Minneapolis. We cannot do that.—*Movement of Destiny*, page 368.

Turning to the R&H article of April 11, 1893 as quoted above, it will be noted that the Ellen G. White statement cited *is less than one-fourth of a sentence*. Can it be possible that in this fragment of a sentence she contradicts the clear and consistent teaching of Holy Scripture and the balanced import of dozens of her other statements in context? It is important to look at the article in context, citing passages that show the true thought of the article. Then the mutilated sentence must be noted in its entirety, intact in italics and which was written after the "revivals" took place and most of the "confessions" came in:

> O how few know the day of their visitation! ... How few there are who are truly humble, devoted, God-fearing servants in the cause of Christ. ... Today there are few who are heartily serving God. The most of those who compose our congregations are spiritually dead in trespasses and sin. ... The sweetest melodies that come from God through human lips—justification by faith, and the righteousness of Christ [the 1888 message] —do not bring forth from them a response of love and gratitude. ... They steel their hearts against [Christ] make a profession, but deny the power of true godliness. ... What more can I say than I have said to impress upon our churches, and especially upon the church at Battle Creek [the church leadership], the eternal loss they are liable to in not arousing and putting to use the executive ability that God has given them? ... How many more messages of reproof and warning must the Lord send to His chosen people before they will obey? ... The people have been convinced that they should be laborers together with God, but have they been converted to the idea? ... It has been clearly shown that in the righteousness of Christ is our only hope of gaining access to the Father. ... Would greater evidence, more powerful manifestations, break down the barriers that have been interposed between the truth and the soul? —No. I have been shown that sufficient evidence has been given. Those who reject the evidence already presented would not be convinced by more abundant proof. They are like the Jews. ... Often the outward manifestation of selfishness is done away for a time, but its hateful fruit will again appear as do the leaves of a tree that has been cut down, but whose root remains. If a fiber of selfishness is left, it will spring forth again, and bear a harvest after its kind. ... The Lord is at work seeking to purify His people, and this great work is retarded by unbelief and stubbornness. ... Light has been shining upon the church of God, but many have said by their indifferent attitude, "We want not Thy way, O Lord, but our own way." ... Think how great light was given to the Jews, and yet they

rejected the Lord of Life and glory. ... There is less excuse in our day for stubbornness and unbelief than there was for the Jews in the days of Christ. ... Many say, "If I had only lived in the days of Christ, I would not have wrested His words, or ... rejected and crucified Him as did the Jews," but that will be proved by the way in which you deal with His message [1888] and His messengers today. ... Those who declare that if they had lived in the days of Christ, they would not do as did the rejectors of His mercy, will today be tested. *Those who live in this day are not accountable for the deeds of those who crucified the Son of God; but if with all the light that shone upon His ancient people, delineated before us, we travel over the same ground, cherish the same spirit, refuse to receive reproof and warning, then our guilt will be greatly augmented, and the condemnation that fell upon them will fall upon us, only it will be as much greater as our light is greater in this age than was their light in their age.*—Ellen G. White, R&H, April 4 and 11, 1893.

The context is very clear. In a similar way the word of Ezekiel 18:4 and 20 cannot be used to contradict the numerous texts that call for one generation of leadership to confess and repent because of the sins of their "fathers." Ezekiel is talking about individual sins which are not inherited legally or genetically. For us to recognize that the Church leadership of a previous generation rejected the "beginning of the Latter Rain," and thus delayed the coming of Christ for many decades, is an entirely different matter! Church leadership affects "the body." It is more than individual responsibility.

When church leadership is carefully weighed it need not be considered so impossible and strange that the leadership of eighty years ago rejected the truth of the 1888 message. Sacred history is abundantly clear that it was the leadership, the priests and rulers that rejected Christ at His first coming and thus deceived the people and led to their rejection of the Saviour. Men dare not seek counsel of men to know eternal truth. When the tragedy of that experience dawned upon the hearts of God's people, they were pricked and cried, "What shall we do? " The answer was clear, "Repent! " The heavenly illumination, the divine power that followed made hearts understand truths that had heretofore been uncomprehended. Light broke forth! A faith and assurance sprung up that never had been known before. At the end of time, this *and more* must be accomplished. (See AA 35-46.)

(f) *What can arouse the Church to complete harmony with Heaven in Christ's final work of atonement?* The Church needs a true motivation. The one that alone can do it is concern for *Christ's vindication* rather than selfish concern for personal salvation. If as Ellen G. White says, "The disappointment of Christ is beyond description," something should be done to ease that disappointment He feels. It is not fair to Him to perpetuate His sorrow:

> Few give thought to the suffering that sin has caused our Creator. All Heaven suffered in Christ's agony; but that suffering did not begin or end with His manifestation in humanity. The cross is a revelation to our dull senses of the pain that, from its very inception, sin has brought to the heart of God.—*Education*, page 263.

There are literally scores of statements from the Spirit of Prophecy to the effect that 1888 and its aftermath, as well as the *result* of the 1901 Conference, were a keen disappointment and sorrow to our Lord. The God of Heaven, Ellen G. White says, was "ashamed." "My grief is the same as Christ's was [concerning 1888] ... Every arrow in His quiver is exhausted. ... It is something beyond anything I have ever seen in all my experience since I first entered in the work." (See Letter, May 31, 1896, and MS. 2, 1890.)

If ever a people on earth needed a "final atonement," it is "we." But our popular understanding of the significance of our history, past and current, leaves no room for such a need. We plead for the sake of Christ, to come to a knowledge of the truth and let *us* seek and experience that "final atonement!"

5. *We confess our complete confidence in the triumph of the Seventh-day Adventist Church and the eventual denominational repentance for which we plead.* The only question is, when? Both Scripture and the Spirit of Prophecy writings foretell a glorious denominational repentance which will make possible the finishing of God's work and the coming of the Lord. That which was previously unconscious in history becomes open to perception and understanding. "I will pour upon the house of David [the leadership] and upon the inhabitants of Jerusalem [the church] the spirit of grace and of supplications: and they shall look upon Me whom they have pierced. ... In that day there shall be a fountain opened to the house of David and to the inhabitants of Jerusalem for sin and for uncleanness." Zechariah 12:10; 13:1. Ellen G. White's allusions to this marvelous experience as yet future are numerous. Adventists should know of "the great reformatory movement among God's people" witnessed "in visions of the night" (9T 126) and the "What Might Have Been" chapter of 8T 104-106, and the thrilling meeting seen in vision

described in the *Review and Herald* of February 4, 1902. *These things will come!* The question is—when?

6. *We confess our hearty appreciation of the glorious truths of the 1888 message itself as found in original out-of-print sources that we have had the privilege to see first-hand.* As far back as 1938 we chanced on a copy of E. J. Waggoner's book on Galatians, *The Glad Tidings* (Oakland: Pacific Press, 1900. See *Movement of Destiny*, pages 189, 200, 201.) Never before had we read anything quite so simple, clear and beautiful in explaining Paul's idea of the gospel. And yet we had not an inkling of who the mysterious, and to us, unknown author might be, nor had we even heard of "1888" or the beginning of the Latter Rain at that time. But we felt about Waggoner's book quite as John Wesley felt when he first heard Luther on Galatians: "I did feel my heart strangely warmed." Ignorant that Ellen G. White had once said that "the Lord in His great mercy sent a most precious message to His people" through Elder E. J. Waggoner, we nevertheless recognized it immediately as indeed "most precious." We copied as much of the rare book as we could on an old typewriter, thinking we might never again see one. We have "tasted" and seen that it is good! We are constrained to think that other sinners like ourselves will find a most precious message therein.

7. *We confess ourselves to be the least and most unworthy of all the Lord's servants.* We have not an iota of superior wisdom or goodness. We have nothing and are nothing except by the grace of Christ. We have simply *seen* something that others have not seen. We are not necessarily guilty of the "sheer stubbornness" which *Movement of Destiny* charges upon us because we insist that we have seen what we have seen (page 686, No. 14). The most lowly person can see something! We would not be worthy of the eyes the Lord gave us unless we testified of what we have seen.

What we have seen is not by any special inspiration or revelation, but simply with our own eyes as we have read the 1888 message itself. It is strength for our souls. We believe it is of God. We believe its basic ideas were and will become again "the beginning of the Latter Rain and the Loud Cry." We have *seen* what the servant of the Lord actually said about how it was received by a previous generation of Church leadership. Further, we have *seen* that what we are commonly presenting to the world today lacks that "most precious message," and that because of our reading the Spirit of Prophecy with a "vail" upon our heart we have failed to discern this hidden lack. Our Laodicean pride has made us truly "blind" as our Lord has faithfully said. We have *seen* that His words are really true.

What can we do other than to tell what we have seen?

And then, having seen, point with joy to our Lord's own inspired and wonderful solution, "Be zealous therefore, and *repent*"?

All this we confess!

Donald K. Short   Robert J. Wieland

October, 1972

APPENDICES

APPENDIX A

THE NEW TESTAMENT BASIS OF CORPORATE GUILT AND REPENTANCE

The Apostle Paul takes his stand with these Old Testament writers. He taught the same principle of corporate identity. To Paul, all who believe are the "body of Christ." The church is the "Isaac" of faith, "one body" or *one person* with Abraham and all true believers of all ages (the Greek word *soma* means not only *body* but also *person*). To Gentile as well as Jewish believers Abraham is "our father." See Romans 4:1-13. To the Gentile believers of his day, Paul speaks of "*our* fathers ... all baptized unto Moses," "*we*, being many are one bread, and one body" or one person. See 1 Cor. 10:1-17. "By one spirit are we *all* baptized into one body [person], whether we be Jews or Gentiles, whether we be bond or free; and have been *all* made to drink into one Spirit." "We *all*" means both *past* generations and the *present* generation. Christ's "body" is *all* who have believed in Him from the time of Adam down to the last "remnant" who welcome Him at His second coming. All are "one" corporate individual or person in the pattern of Paul's thinking. The moment we believe we become a part of that corporate person or "body" composed of the saints of all ages, each individual member as closely connected with all other members as the various organs of the human body being separate are yet one corporate entity. See 1 Cor. 12:13-27.

So deeply imbedded in Paul's mind was this Hebrew idea of corporate personhood that he used a unique example to explain it: Levi "payed tithes in Abraham", he said. He was talking about the time when Abraham, *not Levi*, paid *his* tithes to Melchizedek, following the Battle of Siddim before Levi's grandfather Isaac had even been born! How then could *Levi* have paid tithes to Melchizedek? It makes sense only when one recognizes the Hebrew principle of corporate identity: "He was yet in the loins of his [great-grand] father [Abraham], when Melchizedek met him." Heb. 7:9, 10.

The point of Paul's idea is tremendous. The "members" of Christ's "body" are related to each other as the various organs of our physical body are related. When God looks upon the church, He sees more than a mere scattered mass of unrelated individuals. When you think of a friend, you do not envisage an anatomical collection of organs, cells, and limbs; you think of a *person*.

So, says Paul, the Church in all ages is "one person." "If one member suffer, all the members suffer with it; or one member be honoured, all the members rejoice with it." When one "member" falls into sin, all the "members" share the pain and the guilt. No "schism" (1 Cor. 12:25) creates an isolated self-righteousness on the part of any. No generation of the Church says, "Those of us who live today are not accountable for the sins of our spiritual ancestors" (see *Movement of Destiny*, page 368). Such generation self-righteousness would be a "schism" in Paul's idea. Unless specific repentance is experienced for those "sins of our spiritual ancestors," we cannot cut ourselves off from full fellowship with them. In Bible terminology *"Israel" is one individual through all the ages of her national existence.* "Thy birth and thy nativity is of the land of Canaan," the Lord says to Israel of old, addressing her as one woman. Ezekiel 16:3. He reviews her "life-story" through her time of ripening girlhood ("thou wast exceeding beautiful," verse 13, the days of Israel's glory under David and Solomon to her time of mature womanhood when she proved unfaithful to her Divine Lover ("Wherefore, O harlot, hear the word of the Lord," verse 35).

What does this tremendous truth mean to us today? "Our" "birth and ... nativity" was 1844. We, the Seventh-day Adventist Church, are a "woman." Our "babyhood" was the time of pre-organization infancy from 1844 to 1863 when our General Conference was "organized." Our years of "youth" were our years of denominational pride in the 1870s and 1880s when we rejoiced in our invincibility in argumentative debate and our burgeoning institutional growth. Our 1888 "confrontation" was our "time of love" when the Heavenly Bridegroom appealed to "us" to yield our all to Him. The "wedding" would have come in that generation had "we" yielded! "We" were mature and responsible when "we" rejected the "beginning of the Latter Rain" that would have led to the finishing of God's work in that generation and the coming of the Lord.

It is apparent that the oft-repeated remonstrance, "We cannot repent for the mistakes of a previous generation! " is meaningless. It discloses a failure to grasp Bible teaching regarding the realities of human nature.

Jesus Himself experienced corporate repentance. This is evident from both Scripture and the Spirit of Prophecy writings.

Peter says of Him that He "did no sin, neither was guile found in His mouth." 1 Peter 2:22. When John the Baptist baptized Him, it was because Jesus asked for it and insisted on it. If "John verily baptized with the baptism of repentance" (Acts 19:4), he must have baptized Jesus with the only baptism he was capable of administering—a baptism indicating on the part of the sinless Candidate an experience of repentance.

But how could Christ experience repentance if He had never sinned? This is basically the same question often asked, "How can we repent of Calvary and of 1888 if we weren't even born then?" If it is shocking to imagine that good people can repent, it seems incomprehensible that a *perfect* and *sinless* Christ could repent.

The answer is that Jesus, in taking upon Himself our human nature, became a part of the human race and took our sins upon Himself though He was not personally guilty of any of them. The only kind of repentance a sinless person could experience would be a perfect *corporate* repentance. Jesus' experience of repentance is a model and example of what we ourselves should experience.

It is unthinkable that Jesus was suggesting that they act out a play, when He told John at the Jordan, "Thus it becometh us to fulfill all righteousness." Playacting could never "fulfill all righteousness." Our Divine Example could never condone baptism without an appropriate, genuine, and sincere experience of heart. For Him to submit to "the baptism of repentance" without repentance would have been an example of sheer hypocrisy.

His submission to baptism indicates that "the Lord ... laid on Him the iniquity of us all" then and there. His baptism became an injection of healing-repentance for sin into the "body" of humanity. This perfect identity with us began long before Calvary. Ellen G. White offers these perceptive comments on how Christ experienced a deep heart-repentance on our behalf:

> John had heard of the sinless character and spotless purity of Christ. ... John had also seen that He should be the example for every repenting sinner. ... John could not understand why the only sinless one upon the earth should ask for an ordinance implying guilt, virtually confession, by symbol of baptism, pollution to be washed away. ...
>
> Christ came not confessing His own sins; but guilt was imputed to Him as the sinner's substitute. He came not to repent on His own account; but in behalf of the sinner. ... As their substitute. He takes upon Him their sins, numbering Himself with the transgressors, taking

the steps the sinner is required to take; and doing the work the sinner must do.—R&H, January 21, 1873.

After Christ had taken the necessary steps in repentance, conversion, and faith in behalf of the human race. He went to John to be baptized of him in Jordan.—Ellen G. White, *General Conference Bulletin*, 1901, page 36.

Christ ... had taken the steps which every sinner must take, in conversion, repentance, and baptism. He Himself had no sins of which to repent, and therefore He had no sins to wash away. But He was our example in all things, and therefore He must do that which He would have us do.—ST, March 12, 1912; *That I May Know Him*, page 252.

Accordingly, analyze these statements:

(a) Though sinless, Christ did experience repentance.

(b) He knows how the sinner feels, including "every repenting sinner." He put Himself in his place. In our self-righteousness we cannot feel such empathy with "every repenting sinner" because only a Perfect Man can experience perfect repentance.

(c) Christ is our Example in corporate repentance. Who is more holy than He? Lukewarm impenitence comes from either not seeing Him clearly revealed, or from rejecting Him. Jesus' perfect compassion for every human soul is the direct result of His experiencing a perfect repentance in behalf of every soul. He becomes the true "second Adam," partaking of the "body," becoming one with us. Thus He had phenomenal power to win the hearts of sinners. In this pre-baptism experience of "repentance, conversion, and faith in behalf of the human race" Jesus learned to know what was "in man." John 2:25. Only thus could He have learned to speak as "never man spake." John 7:46. We will never as a people learn to love as Jesus loved until we learn to repent as He repented. If Jesus learned to realize His personal involvement with the sin of the whole world, can we be more holy than He and refuse to see it?

This kind of repentance is the path to Christlike love. It effectually conquers lukewarmness forever. The "injection" of Christ's repentance produces a love that permeates His "body," the Church. No longer are we hopeless to "reach" sinners in modern times whose particular evil deeds we do not understand and pride ourselves on not committing. Corporate repentance enables us to bridge the gap that at present insulates us from needy souls whom Christ loves, but for whom He can exercise no healing ministry because we as His instruments are "frozen" in corporate impenitence. Like Christ "who did no sin" but knew repentance, we can feel a genuine compassion in behalf of others whose sins we may not personally have committed, either for lack of opportunity or for lack of temptation of equal intensity. Love is freed from the chains of impenitence and immediately goes to work as Jesus did. Of each sinner we say, "There but for the grace of God am I."

When we have such an experience, many sinners will recognize the reality of it, and will respond where today they turn a deaf ear to us.

The repentance Christ calls for is a path that will lead directly into the finishing of the gospel commission in all the world. Here is where this inspired prediction will find its fulfillment:

> Those who wait for the Bridegroom's coming are to say to the people, "Behold your God." The last rays of merciful light, the last message of mercy to be given to the world, is a revelation of His character of love.—COL 415.

Let it be emphasized as clearly and strongly as possible that the call to denominational repentance has nothing to do with confidence or lack of confidence in the personnel of the General Conference leadership of the Church. The authors of this confession maintain a lifelong confidence in the integrity of General Conference leadership and firmly believe today that the Lord will overrule all things for the finishing of His work in triumph, honoring the principles of organization to the very end.

The leadership of the Church and the Church itself are all "one body," one corporate whole. The strengths and weaknesses of one are that of the other. If the actual personnel of leadership were changed a thousand times, the call of our Lord Jesus, "Be zealous therefore, and repent," would still be valid until a denominational repentance is fully effective in preparing for the finishing of the work in all the world. "There is none righteous, no, not one." Romans 3:10. We *all*, without a single exception, need to understand how our Saviour's call is to us.

Therefore it is useless and irrelevant to say that recognizing the facts of our history, past and current, is being "critical." Is Christ "critical"? Certainly not. Yet His message to the Laodicean Church has often been so interpreted by the enemy of God's work.

If when we hear our Lord's call we simply say "Amen!" we are responding in the only way an honest and contrite heart can respond.

APPENDIX B

With all the solemnity connected with this "Confession," yet there may be a place for the thoughts expressed hereunder. For those who *know,* this exhibit may bring a smile and be considered merely as a joke! For anyone who *does not know,* this exhibit might be considered clear-cut historical evidence to definitely establish the validity of the case.

Someone has compiled the following "Fourteen-point Summation" proving that the 'Jews' accepted Christ as the Messiah:

1. "Some" accepted Him. See Acts 17:4; John 1:12.
2. The twelve disciples were all Jews.
3. The Apostle Paul was a Jew.
4. Apollos was a Jew.
5. Jesus Himself was a Jew—and He accepted Himself!
6. The Gospels were all written by Jews, except perhaps Luke.
7. The Jerusalem Church (Jews) predominated.
8. At least two members of the Sanhedrin accepted Christ—Joseph and Nicodemus. This was surely "Some."
9. Gamaliel, a member of the Sanhedrin, did not appose the apostles.
10. "A great company of the priests were obedient to the faith." See Acts 6:7.
11. The New Testament was written entirely by Jews, with the possible exception of Luke.
12. "The common people heard Him gladly." See Mark 12:37.
13. The Jews tried to make Jesus King. John 6:15 (Does that sound like rejection?)
14. "A great multitude ... of the Jews ... believed." Acts 14:1.

APPENDIX C

Following is a sampling of the actual text of *1888 Re-examined*. These direct quotations are taken from the original lengthy 204-page, legal size, document. Sufficient is presented here so that an evaluation can be made of the general tone of this 1950 treatise:

> Every failure of God's people to follow the light shining upon their pathway for the past century must be completely rectified by the present generation before the remnant church can be granted any divine vindication before the world. Absolutely nothing which does not bear the test of truth will be triumphant in the Judgment. As Judge, God simply cannot and will not clear the guilty, whether it be an individual or a movement. If this is true, it follows that there is before the remnant church a heavy account to settle. And the sooner the issue is faced squarely and candidly, the better. ...
>
> Hence the need for thorough investigation, that true history may be distinguished from the "tradition of the elders." For various reasons to be named later, the Minneapolis episode of our history has been enveloped in the foggy mists of that tradition. Fact must be separated from fancy.
>
> The cleansing of the sanctuary can never be complete until the Minneapolis incident of our history is fully understood, and the tragic mistake rectified.—Pages 2, 3.
>
> It must be pointed out... that there never was an issue or tide to be turned with the people; the issue or the tide was entirely with the leaders and the ministry of the movement. The people would gladly have accepted the light had the leaders permitted it to come to them undistorted and unopposed, or rather, had the leaders joined heartily in presenting it. There were many among the younger ministers, even, who were keenly interested in the message presented. They investigated their Bibles, and the message was doubtless a common topic of conversation. But the continually noncommittal attitude, or outright opposition, originating with responsible leaders in Battle Creek and elsewhere, quenched the movement.—Page 29.
>
> The [1888] message being of God in a special sense, the authoritative, responsible, and persistent opposition to it constituted

a spiritual defeat for the Advent movement, which defeat must be recognized merely to be a battle in a larger war, and not the losing of the war itself. Such a view of the matter will require that this generation recognize the facts of the case, and thoroughly rectify the tragic mistake. This can be done, and the living, righteous God will help us.—Page 38.

The true cleansing of the heavenly sanctuary requires a complementary work of cleansing the sub-conscious content of our heart and mind of hidden, buried, "underground" roots of unbelief and enmity against God. Light which will lay bare these spiritual conditions, and a means of spiritual therapy adequate for dealing with them, is more immediately needful than any amount of supernatural power for the propagation of our present "faith." In other words, the *power* which we want is going to be *light*. The finishing of the work will be a natural consequence. A true understanding of Minneapolis [1888] and its aftermath is in line of diagnosis; a true understanding of the Cross is in the line of treatment.—Page 89.

That experience [the "loud cry" power] is yet future for the remnant church, rendered so by her own stubborn unbelief in the past.—Page 94.

After we have gathered up the fragments that remain [of the 1888 message] that nothing be lost, then could we with confidence press our petition to the throne of grace to give us *this* day bread convenient for us, meat in due season. As surely as there is a living God, the prayer would not be unanswered.—Page 120.

'The remnant church, enfeebled and defective as she is, is still the supreme object of His [God's] regard.' The long Detour of wandering which we brought upon ourselves must lead us in the fulness of the time to the Christ whom we spurned at Minneapolis. In self-abhorrence and deep repentance, we shall find Him. There will be no self-vindication in the process. ...

A recognition of the significance of our denominational history in the light of Spirit of Prophecy declarations, is essential before the loud cry can be recognized and received. Could any other kind of "loud cry" than that which would follow a denominational repentance "lighten the earth with glory"? What glory for *God* would there be in it? —Page 137.

The precious talent intended by its Giver to be used for the blessing of the world still lies buried, wrapped in the napkin of neglect.

The present generation of Israel will not spurn and ridicule the presentation of that message, as did the generation of 1888-93, *if* God's confidence in the honesty of Israel as being worthy of the plan of salvation is justified. For us to fail again would compromise the honor of God's throne, for He has staked that honor upon His confidence in the honesty of the Seventh-day Adventist conscience. In a sense, God Himself is now on trial in the course to be pursued by His people. . . .

If *now* [1950] is understood to be the time for the proclamation of the loud cry, it follows that *now* is the time for the making right of the Minneapolis [1888] wrong. The mistake of Minneapolis was the rejection of the very power which the church is now committed to a program of seeking for. ...

Any reproduction of [the 1888] teaching must therefore be considered as only the *beginning* of the light which is needed, while obviously far in advance of our present contemporary understanding. A sincere acceptance of that self-humbling message would be the necessary preparation for the reception of further light to be communicated in God's chosen way, in response to the intelligent prayers of His people.—Pages 202-204.

A CHRONOLOGICAL TABLE OF INTEREST LEADING TO THIS "CONFESSION"

1938	Authors' original unwitting contact with 1888 message through discovery of *The Glad Tidings*, by E. J. Waggoner (a verse-by-verse study on Galatians).
1947	Publication of *The Fruitage of Spiritual Gifts*, Review and Herald Publishing Association. Thesis regarding 1888: the message was merely a re-emphasis of the historic Protestant doctrine as taught by Luther, Wesley, and other Reformers; 1888 message was accepted, great revival, marvelous victory for Church.
1949	Publication of *Captains of the Host*, Review and Herald Publishing Association. Thesis regarding 1888: no recognition that message was beginning of the Latter Rain; initial opposition changed to acceptance; Jones' and Waggoner's message faulty and extreme; 1890s were era of victory. Neither book examines primary sources of information on this subject.
1950	December—Research begins by the authors into the 1888 history, in the Potomac University Library and the Vault of the Ellen G. White Publications office, Washington. Interest sparked by Seminary classes. Initial permission to study Ellen G. White materials in the Vault revoked.
1950	Winter, Spring—Gathering of Ellen G. White manuscripts from retired ministers relevant to the 1888 era.

1950	July—Letter to General Conference Officers concerning so-called "Christ-centered preaching" versus the 1888 concepts of "righteousness by faith." Officers reply, cancelling return bookings to Africa and appointing a hearing in September.
1950	August-Writing of *1888 Re-examined*, and preparation of 204 mimeograph stencils.
1950	September—Hearing before General Conference subcommittee in Washington; presentation of 16 copies of *1888 Re-examined*, to General Conference. Subsequent clearing for return to Africa as missionaries.
1950-1951	Winter—Return to East Africa, resumption of mission service.
1951	December—Manuscript rejected by Defense Literature Committee; authors urged not to disseminate their convictions. Reason for rejection: Authors' evaluation of 1888 message as beginning of the Latter Rain and Loud Cry, new light never fully perceived before, "not true;" their interpretation of the 1888 aftermath wrong, on authority of A. W. Spalding; manuscript is "critical," Holy Spirit now being poured out on Church in "doubling our membership" program; minor theological problems also cited.
1952	February-March—Authors reply to Defense Literature Committee by letter, appeal their decision to judgment of the Lord and the disposition of His providence; write friends not to agitate the issues or republish the manuscript.

1952-1957	While authors are in Africa, unauthorized individuals in different parts of the world reproduce *1888 Re-examined*, for distribution. Some private individuals make or hire stenographers to make personal copies, retyping it in its entirety. Authors receive numerous letters telling how readers greatly blessed in reading it. Correspondents urge General Conference to show real reason why manuscript was rejected in 1951. Pressure results in preparation by the General Conference of another reply to manuscript. Meanwhile, authors maintain confidence in the ultimate triumph of truth and advise loyalty to Church and its organization.
1958	June—Authors attend General Conference Session, Cleveland, peruse advance copy of *A Further Appraisal*, second General Conference reply to the manuscript.
1958	July—Authors write to chairman of committee pointing out fallacies and untenable portions of this document, quoting Ellen G. White evidence, in attempt to save General Conference from embarrassment.
1958	August—Further research, gathering of unpublished Ellen G. White material.
1958	September—General Conference publishes *A Further Appraisal of 1888 Re-examined*, in substantially same form as advance copy seen at Session. Reaffirms its rejection. Reason given was one not even mentioned in 1951 report, in fact was implicitly denied therein: authors had wrested many of their Ellen G. White exhibits from their overall context and thus formed wrong conclusions.
1958	October—Authors send 70-page mimeographed document to General Conference Committee members, *An Answer to A Further Appraisal*. Authors quote Ellen G. White exhibits in larger context. Many unpublished documents not available in 1950 added in support of thesis.

1959	January—Authors again appeal the ultimate disposition of these issues to God's care, assure General Conference of continuing loyalty, return again to East African mission field.
1959	January—Officers receive Third Report from subcommittee appointed to deal with the manuscript. No discussion of evidence contained in authors' *An Answer*.
1959	Authors grant permission to concerned layman to appeal consideration of *1888 Re-examined* to North Pacific Union Committee, through regular channels. Appeal results in laymember publishing an edition of facsimile-reproduced documents pro and con, including original manuscript together with various General Conference refutations.
1961	April—General Conference President invites authors to submit in writing a brief summary of their manuscript for further consideration by a subcommittee of five.
1961	July-Brief summary written and submitted by mail, from East Africa. General Conference withholds from the authors the identity of the five members of this Committee.
1961	August—Anonymous committee of five reports to General Conference President. General Conference withholds reports from the authors of *1888 Re-examined*, sends only selected excerpts. Authors are told that the judgment of this anonymous committee is against their manuscript. This should end the matter.

1962	February—Publication of *By Faith Alone*, Pacific Press Publishing Association. Written at General Conference request as an effective answer to the basic thesis of *1888 Re-examined*. Thesis regarding 1888 message: was same as the message of justification as taught in the creeds of the Protestant churches of the day; no clear recognition that it was the beginning of the Latter Rain; message since 1888 "in perfect harmony with the best evangelical teaching"—fails to distinguish between popular Evangelical "righteousness by faith" and that which is in harmony with the cleansing of the sanctuary and which will make possible the final atonement; rejects denominational repentance.
1964-1971	Author of *Movement of Destiny* corresponds with authors of *1888 Re-examined*, offers to share evidence that will disprove their thesis. Authors ask to be allowed to see relevant Ellen G. White evidence. Request denied, authors told they will see evidence in forthcoming book, urged to retract before publication seriously embarrasses them. Authors reply that they can retract only when they themselves see the relevant Ellen G. White evidence requiring such a retraction.
1966	March-Publication of *Through Crisis to Victory, 1888-1901*, endorsed by Ellen G. White Estate as an answer to the thesis of *1888 Re-examined*.
1967	June—One of the authors of *1888 Re-examined* invited to meet with subcommittee in Washington to discuss implications of the manuscript and its circulation by unauthorized publishers. Basic thesis of manuscript again rejected, this time on the grounds that it has contributed to a breakdown of confidence in General Conference leadership. Author denies this charge, iterates that such breakdown of confidence stems rather from untenable nature of positions taken to counteract call to denominational repentance.

1969	Publication of *The Faith That Saves*. Thesis regarding 1888: completely fails to recognize real significance of the message as being beginning of the Latter Rain; discounts value of Jones and Waggoner contribution; true righteousness by faith is taught by evangelical Protestantism; the 1926 General Conference messages deserve more study than the 1888 message. (Investigation of the 1926 messages reveals that in general they were identical to the popular Evangelical presentations of the day and did not include the fundamental basics of the 1888 message.)
1969	May—*Review and Herald* (May 8) publishes article, "The Year 1888," reporting on results of June 1967 meeting; General Conference affirms confidence in loyalty and sincerity of authors of *1888 Re-examined*.
1971	February—Publication of *Movement of Destiny*.
1971	May—First presentation of church "Week of Prayer," using slides photographed from out-of-print 1888 message sources. Title of series: "The 1888 Message Itself as Found in the Writings of Jones and Waggoner."
1971-1972	December-January—Editorials in the *Review and Herald* affirming the basic 1888 view of Christ's nature in incarnation.
1972	March—First publication in an official denominational publication (*The Ministry*) of recommendation to study writings of Jones and Waggoner.
1972	October—Publication of a re-print of *The Glad Tidings* as revised and edited by one of the authors (Pacific Press Publishing Association).
1972	October—Completion of *"An Explicit Confession ... Due the Church"* by the authors of *1888 Re-examined*.

ABOUT THE AUTHORS

Both were born into non-Seventh-day Adventist homes. Both took their stand and became Seventh-day Adventists by study and conviction and were baptized in their youth while attending public high school. Each has been in continuous denominational service for over 30 years with an aggregate of over 50 years in foreign mission service and each is at present serving in his appointed place carrying ministerial credentials of the Seventh-day Adventist Church. Details of service over the years will be found in the relative issues of the Seventh-day Adventist Yearbook.

Donald K. Short was born in Indiana. As a result of attending a series of evangelistic tent meetings in Daytona Beach, Florida, he was baptized into the Seventh-day Adventist Church in 1930, during his second year in high school. His subsequent education was all in denominational schools, Forest Lake Academy, Southern Junior College, graduating from Columbia Union College in 1940, with the bachelor's degree. While in college he earned a living operating a private printing business. He was also connected with various evangelistic meetings from the time he became an Adventist and in the fall of 1940 sailed for Africa to serve at Mbeya Mission, Tanganyika. He remained in East Africa until 1960, serving as training school principal, educational secretary, mission director and publishing house manager during this time. Since 1960, he has served as general manager of the Trans-Africa Division publishing house, Sentinel Publishing Association, located in Cape Town, Republic of South Africa. He holds the master of arts degree from Andrews University (1959).

Robert J. Wieland was born in Iowa and became a Seventh-day Adventist in Florida in 1929, largely as the result of personal Bible study while attending the Presbyterian Sunday School. The only Adventist boy at that time in the local high school, he went through the experience of having to stand alone for Sabbath observance before students and teachers. Academic and musical achievements resulted in pressure from school administration to participate in various functions on Sabbath. Graduating in theology from Columbia Union College in 1939, with the bachelor's degree, he entered denominational service in the Florida Conference, serving as a pastor until called to Kakoro Mission, East Africa, in 1944. Before sailing for Africa he was ordained to the ministry in the Florida Conference. He served as president of the Uganda and

Central Kenya Missions, Voice of Prophecy secretary for the East African Union, and book and periodical editor of the East African Publishing House, until return to America in 1965. Since then he has been a pastor in the South-eastern California Conference, at present serving the Chula Vista Church in the San Diego area. He holds the master of arts degree in theology from Andrews University (1965).

SUBJECT INDEX

Anthology of Jones' and Waggoner's writings, 4
Apology and retraction, do authors owe the Church? 7
Atonement,
    final, desperate need for, 4, 5
    relation to denomination repentance, 35
    supplies effective motivation, 45
Cleansing of sanctuary, 5
Christ,
    honour and vindication involved in Seventh-day Adventist history, 5, 28, 36
    repentance and baptism of, 48-50
    true versus false, 5
Chronological table of *1888 Re-examined*, 65-70
Dead, "impeachment of," 7, 24
1888 history,
    called a "standstill," 17
    confessions of those who rejected message, 20-24
    eyewitness reports, 20-21
    "facts are accessible," 3, 25
    God has been with the Church ever since 1888, 19
    post-1888 administration provides decisive evidence for, 7-17
1888 message,
    distinct from popular Evangelical concepts of righteousness by faith, 36, 37, 41-43
    "some" accepted, "some" rejected—significance of, 11, 18, 40
    trial presentation of, 1971, 38
    would have been gladly accepted by Church, 15
1888 Re-examined,
    cited, 7, 19, 24
    chronological table of history of, 65-70
    excerpts from, Appendix C, 62-64
    holding to its thesis is "sheer stubbornness," 35, 53
    prepared for General Conference Committee, 1

600 Ellen G. White exhibits used in, 1, 15
    Synopsis of basic thesis, 4-6, 36
Facts "accessible," must be seen by all, 3, 4, 15
Final atonement, 5, 39, 45, 52
"Few," the "some" who accepted the 1888 message were, 5, 11, 40
General Conference Committee,
    confession of, 1897, 17
    confidence of authors in, 50, 51
    lead in denominational repentance, 6
    of Nineveh, 45
The Glad Tidings, by E. J. Waggoner, 53
Guilt, corporate, distinguished from inherited or legal, 46
History, denominational, clear call to denominational repentance, 14, 25, 32
Jews, "our" opposition to 1888 message like their rejection of Christ, 50
Kadesh-Barnea, 19, 22-24
Latter Rain and Loud Cry,
    1888 message beginning of, 1, 2, 4, 5, 6, 26, 27, 34
    none of initial rejectors ever had part in, 22, 23
    repentance for rejecting, 47, 48, 49
Love,
    can never be experienced as Christ experienced, until we repent as He repented, 59
    can never permeate Church without final Atonement, 5
    General Conference leadership lost first love after 1888, 18
    "what might have been," at 1901 Session, 31
Loyalty, both for Christ and the Church, 5
Motivation, true Christ-centered necessary, 5, 52
1901 General Conference Session, "victory," 25-30
Reject, rejection, how Ellen G. White used synonymous terms, 6, 13, 18, 21, 30, 46, 50, 51
Repentance, corporate,
    Christ's experience of, 57-59
    definition of, 47, 59
    New Testament basis of, Appendix A, 56-60
    only remedy for lukewarmness, 41, 46
Repentance, denominational, 6, 7, 14, 35, 44, 45
    assurance that it will come, 53
    call to rejected, 40, 41, 50

    Christ appealed for from Jewish nation, 45
    definition of, 47
    1901 Conference failed to experience, 27
    Nineveh an example of, 45
Review and Herald, affirms loyalty of authors, 2
"Some" who accepted or rejected 1888 message, clarified, 5, 7, 18, 40, 50
Unconscious, enmity against God, 5
Unity, what alone can bring, 11
Unpublished Ellen G. White material regarding 1888 history, how authors obtained, 15, 26, 65, 67
"Victory," 1901 Conference, 26, 28, 31
Vindication of Christ involved in Seventh-day Adventist history, 5, 32-34, 41, 51
"Wieland and Short ... support organization and unity of Church," 2

BIBLIOGRAPHY

BOOKS

Christian, Lewis Harrison, *The Fruitage of Spiritual Gifts*. Washington: Review and Herald Publishing Association, 1947.

Daniells, Arthur G., *Christ Our Righteousness*. Washington: Review and Herald Publishing Association, 1941.

Froom, Leroy Edwin, *The Fascinating Story of Movement of Destiny*. Washington: Review and Herald Publishing Association, (undated).

—, *Movement of Destiny*. Washington: Review and Herald Publishing Association, 1971.

Jones, Alonzo Trevier, *The Consecrated Way to Christian Perfection*. Mountain View: Pacific Press Publishing Association, 1905.

Olson, A. V., *Through Crisis to Victory 1888-1901*. Washington: Review and Herald Publishing Association, 1966.

Pease, Norval F., *By Faith Alone*. Mountain View: Pacific Press Publishing Association, 1962.

—, *The Faith That Saves*. Washington: Review and Herald Publishing Association, 1969.

Spalding, Arthur Whitefield, *Captains of the Host*. Washington: Review and Herald Publishing Association, 1949.

—, *Origin and History of Seventh-day Adventists*, Vols. Two and Three. Washington: Review and Herald Publishing Association, 1962.

Waggoner, E. J., *Christ and His Righteousness*. Oakland: Pacific Press Publishing Association, 1890 (facsimile reprint, Nashville: Southern Publishing Association, 1972).

—, *The Glad Tidings*. Oakland: Pacific Press Publishing Association, 1900.

—, *The Gospel in Creation*, Battle Creek: Review and Herald Publishing Association, 1894.

White, Ellen G., *Acts of the Apostles*, Mountain View: Pacific Press Publishing Association, 1911.

—, *Counsels to Writers and Editors*, Nashville: Southern Publishing Association, 1946.

—, *Desire of Ages*, Mountain View: Pacific Press Publishing Association, 1898.

—, *Education*, Mountain View: Pacific Press Publishing Association, 1903.

—, *Patriarchs and Prophets*, Mountain View: Pacific Press Publishing Association, 1913.

—, *Selected Messages*, Books I, II. Washington: Review and Herald Publishing Association, 1958.

—, *Seventh-day Adventist Bible Commentary*. Washington: Review and Herald Publishing Association, 1956. Vol. 5.

—, *Testimonies for the Church*. Mountain View: Pacific Press Publishing Association, 1904. Vols. V, VIII, IX.

—, *Testimonies to Ministers*. Mountain View: Pacific Press Publishing Association, 1923.

PUBLICATIONS

General Conference Bulletin, 1893.
Review and Herald, March 18, 1890; May 27, 1890;
    November 22, 1892; April 4, 11, 1893; December 15, 1904;
    November 17, 1910; May 8, 1969.

MANUSCRIPTS AND LETTERS

Jones, Alonzo Trevier, Letter to Claude Holmes, May 12, 1921.
McReynolds, C, *Experiences While at the General Conference in Minneapolis, Minn., in 1888.*
Nash, R. T., *An Eyewitness Report of the 1888 General Conference at Minneapolis.*
Waggoner, E. J., *Confession of Faith*, published letter, 1916.
White, Ellen G., letter, August 20, 1892; letter, August 30, 1892;
    letter, January 9, 1893; letter, February 2, 1896;
    letter, May 31, 1896; letter, August 27, 1896;
    letter, September 19, 1896; letter, July 27, 1897;
    letter, unedited remarks in College Library, April 1, 1901;
    letter, August 5, 1902; letter, August 11, 1902;
    letter, January 2, 1903; letter, January 15, 1903;
    letter, W-58, 1906.

ADDENDUM

Some who have read the pre-publication proofs of this "Confession" have suggested that readers may find difficulty in grasping what we mean by the terms "corporate guilt" and "corporate repentance." Lest any get a wrong impression we are adding this postscript to set forth in some inspired terminology just what is the heart-experience to which we are referring. While we feel that "corporate" is the only English term that can represent Paul's idea of the "body" or "person" relationship the Church bears, other Biblical terms have at times been used that speak of this underlying "thou-knowest-not" guilt and corresponding repentance which is appropriate:

As the prophet Isaiah beheld the glory of the Lord, he was amazed, and, overwhelmed with a sense of his own weakness and unworthiness, he cried, "Woe is me! for I am undone; because I am a man of unclean lips, and I dwell in the midst of a people of unclean lips." ... Now he sees himself exposed to the same condemnation he had pronounced upon [others]. ... When our eyes look by faith into the sanctuary, and take in the reality, the importance and holiness, of the work there being done, everything of a selfish nature will be abhorred by us. Sin will appear as it is,—the transgression of God's holy law. The atonement will be better understood. ...

The vision given to Isaiah represents the condition of God's people in the last days. They are privileged to see by faith the work that is going forward in the heavenly sanctuary. ... As they look by faith into the holy of holies, ... they perceive that they are a people of unclean lips. ... Well may they despair as they contrast their own weakness and unworthiness with the purity and loveliness of the glorious character of Christ. But if they will humble their souls before God, there is hope for them. ... The work done for Isaiah will be performed in them.—Ellen G. White, *Review and Herald*, December 22, 1896.

This fearful message [to the Laodiceans] will do its work. ... It is designed to arouse the people of God, to discover to them their backslidings, and to lead to zealous repentance, that they may be favored with the presence of Jesus, and be fitted for the loud cry of the third angel.—1T 186.

Sometime it [the full post-1888 story] will be seen in its true bearing, with all the burden of woe that has resulted from it.—Ellen G. White, *General Conference Bulletin*, 1893, p. 184.

There will be a great humbling of hearts before God on the part of every one who remains faithful and true to the end.—Ellen G. White, sermon at Minneapolis, 1888, *Through Crisis to Victory*, p. 297.